WOOF!

A Gay Man's Guide to Dogs

BY ANDREW DePRISCO • Illustrations by Jason O'Malley

Karla Austin *Business Operations Manager*
Barbara Kimmel *Managing Editor*
Amy Deputato *Senior Editor*
Jessica Knott *Production Supervisor*
Sherise Buhagiar *Graphic Layout*
Bill Jonas *Designer*

Library of Congress Cataloging-in-Publication Data

DePrisco, Andrew.
Woof!: a gay man's guide to dogs / by Andrew DePrisco; illustrations by Jason O'Malley.
p. cm.
ISBN-13: 978-1-931993-86-9 (alk. paper)
ISBN-10: 1-931993-86-6 (alk. paper)
1. Dogs. 2. Dogs—Selection. 3. Dog breeds. 4. Gay men—Humor. 5. Gay wit and humor. I. Title.

SF426.D43 2007
636.7—dc22

2006038889

BowTie Press®
A division of BowTie Inc.
3 Burroughs
Irvine, California 92618

Printed and bound in Singapore
First printing in 2007:

12 11 10 09 08 07 1 2 3 4 5 6 7 8 9 10

Dedication

To Tengu, my favorite boy and a wondrous Shiba Inu,
To the memory of the ever-smiling Kabuki,
To the scene-stealing Azuki, our show girl,
To Max, the dog who tracked down my heart, and
To Max's owner, Robert, the center of my world.

Le WOOF

Contents

Acknowledgments 6

Prelude: The Max Factor 7

It's a Fabulous Life! 8

Choosing a Canine Partner 14

A Rainbow of Purebred Dogs 24

The Gay Group System 42

Matchmaker: A–Z 56

And Puppy Makes Three 114

A Major Fabulous Purchase 120

Enter the Family Dog 134

The Other End of the Rainbow Leash 156

Studs and Bitches: The Secret Sex Lives of Dogs 168

Sharing Your Life 176

The Rainbow Tour: Stepping Out in Gay Society 188

Acknowledgments

A book as warped as this one shouldn't be pinned on one poor contracted individual. Were it not for the gentle prodding of a number of sadistic colleagues, I could never have sunken to the depths of this present volume. Surely BowTie's own Operations Manager Karla Austin deserves the first round of "woofs." Thanks for her encouragement and support, nudging and nipping all of us like an alpha Border Collie on Ritalin.

Among my cheering section—"They're actually going to publish this?"—are my dearest friends: Felix Truex, David Wichman, Gabrielle Stravelli, Angelina Villapiano, Michael Monks, Ann Marie Freda, and Aldo Suarez.

Thanks to my many proofreaders and sounding boards, including the aforementioned and twice-blessed Felix Truex, Allan Reznik, Dawne Deeley, Christine Kephart, and Art Stickney, who I believe is still looking for the perfect title.

So many top dog men—are they *really* all tops?—came forward to help me with this project; without their insight, good humor, and dog-world experience, *Woof!* would have been a hollow howl. My thanks to Gary Bachman, Bo Bengtson, David Fitzpatrick, Doug Johnson, and Lloyd Alton and Bill Gorodner. My litany of thanks continues to all of my contributors: Greg Castillo and David Bueno, Jerome "Jero" Cushman, Dr. Samuel Draper, Don Emslie and Tim Doxtater, Bill Ferrara, Richard Gebhardt and John Bannon, Steve Leyerly and Bill Shelton, Ken Matthews and Wayne Miller, Billy Miller and Kenny Saenz, David Murray, Thom Parrotti, Tray Pittman and Paul Flores, Dr. John Reeve-Newson and Dr. Richard Meen, Frank Sabella, William Secord, Ken Sinclair, Tom Stark, Randy Tincher and Johnnie Roe, Richard Tomita and William Scolnik, Dick Yoho and Steve Houser, and Raymond Yurick and Shawn Nichols.

Special thanks to the Woof Fan Club, each of whom has promised to claw their way to the front of the line to buy this book (if I mentioned their names): Betty-Anne Stenmark, Patricia Trotter, Muriel P. Lee, Bardi McLennan, Christine Carter, Barbara J. Andrews, Nona Kilgore Bauer, Jan Grebe, Amy Fernandez, John Merriman and Bill Tacke, Nikki Moustaki, Margaret Logreira, Caterina O'Sullivan, and Suzanne Orban-Stagle Readmond.

To the talented and patient editorial and production staff at BowTie, especially Amy Deputato, Barbara Kimmel, Jarelle Stein, Sherise Buhagiar, and Bill Jonas.

A giant thank you to my illustrator, Jason O'Malley, whose colorful creations would be my reason for purchasing this book.

And to Robert White, for sharing my love of life and love of dogs. This one's for you.

Prelude: The Max Factor

I owe my current relationship with Robert to a Vizsla named Max. In 1997, Robert was crafty enough to use his untrained (wild!) hunting dog to track me down. Robert had been hunting me for years, I discovered, but with no success until Max.

After listening to Robert's accounts of the puppy's complete lack of discipline and being frightened by his owner's textbook training faux pas, I decided to meet the four-month-old Hungarian monster face to face.

The first three hours of my visit I spent with my hand and forearm in Max's mouth. Almost nothing is as oral as a bird dog who's teething.

Even though Robert had been an acquaintance for some time prior, the evening that we shared with Max was the first time we ever really connected. As clueless (and handsome) as Robert was, I discovered a nurturing, vulnerable side to him that I hadn't seen before. He was trying to be Max's guardian, friend, and hero.

By 1997, I had been working in the dog business for ten years and had some experience with dog training and showing. I offered some free advice on behavior and how not to train a bird-brained, obsessive pointing dog.

Robert wasn't really interested in the asset of my dog knowledge, but he asked me out anyway. I resumed Max's education a week later, and they're both in my bed a decade later, considerably well trained.

Find a dog to share your life with: love him, train him, and use him as a decoy whenever gaily possible.

IT'S A FABULOUS LIFE

Once you find your life partner, the world becomes a different place, a better place. When that perfect mate has a soft beard, a wet nose, and four legs, it's even better.

Your new companion doesn't cringe at the word *commitment*, and he lives for you! Day and night, he's always ready for whatever you have in mind, work or play. He can be trained to live by your rules, he can be fun and easy to have around, and he always responds to the *come* command. He doesn't require extravagant gifts or fancy meals, and you can never forget his birthday because he doesn't know that he has one. He even thinks of you as his master.

Inevitably, all your jealous friends will ask how you two met. For once, you don't have to say Match.com or a *Times* personal ad. For once, your involvement with a "breeder" has led to good things! For once, you can be certain that your parents are going to love him—leash, harness, wiggly walk and all.

Choosing a beautiful dog, an impressive dog, a purebred dog is one of life's greatest privileges. Identifying yourself with a breed of dog adds to your own profile. You're no longer just a gay recovering Catholic, French-Filipino Aries power-bottom Bear accountant, now you're a gay recovering Catholic, French-Filipino Aries power-bottom Bear accountant who owns two Lhasa Apsos! (Let's make it perfectly clear from the onset of this book, *Woof!* is not about labels.) Finding the right dog for you, one who will fit into your lifestyle, home, and Ferragamo messenger bag, is part of the noble mission of this book. We will examine your own temperament, living conditions, and needs as well as describe dozens of fabulous purebred dogs for you. Now we move on to the "C" word.

FOR BETTER OR FOR WORSE

Does every gay man *need* a dog? Of course not. Some gay men simply can't handle the responsibility of owning a dog. Some can't commit to a color, much less a living creature. Half of my friends can't keep a philodendron alive, but they're always fantasizing about the perfect Pomeranian being toted about in that fabulous Louis Vuitton dog carrier. Luckily for that poor matted Pom, certain gay people have spared the canine race the abuse and disappointment and have resigned themselves to a dogless existence.

If you have a life—a busy one—you also may not be a candidate for a dog. Even though a pooch will gladly sit at home, waiting for the phone to ring or your Audi to cruise into park—that's no life for a dog. Far more patient and forgiving than your dream boyfriend, a dog will still come running to you after you've stranded him home with nothing more than stale kibble and last month's *Details,* but who'd blame him for breaking out of Fox River State Pen and escaping with Wentworth Miller? Don't imprison your dog. Spare him the lonely boredom, and buy yourself an Amazon parrot or a Hyacinth macaw instead.

If, however, you can envision yourself with a dog; aren't afraid of the commitment, the mess, or the joyful chaos of a puppy; and have the time to invest, you'll discover a whole new world of indescribable companionship. Ask anyone who's known a dog, who's shared his life with a dog: to know a dog is to know "the wet and reckless affection of [his] unconditional love," as novelist Ann Patchett eloquently phrases it. Dogs instinctively care about how you're feeling, need to know what you're doing, and want to be near you. Pulitzer Prize-winning playwright Edward Albee puts it even better: " . . . there are those of us who feel incomplete without the company of a dog or two."* Perhaps you are one of us who need to be completed by a dog!

* Footnote: Edward Albee was interviewed by Neil Plakcy and Sharon Sakson for their wonderful book *Paws and Reflect: Exploring the Bond Between Gay Men and Their Dogs* (2006, Alyson Books).

FAMILY VALUES

Sitcoms in the 1970s certainly didn't help my gay generation learn anything about what constituted a meaningful gay life and family. Although we assumed one of those Brady boys was queer, and we repressed our sexual yearnings for the Professor on *Gilligan's Island,* there were no gay role models to be viewed on the small screen. Even when Tony Randall portrayed a sexless character in his own sitcom in the 1980s, no one actually said that Sidney was a Size Queen who chased Twinks on weekends. He was just a lonely guy, someone's unmarried uncle, bouncing an adorable preadolescent child on his knee.

The silver screen was of minimal help as well. There were a few great gay films, such as *The Sound of Music* and *West Side Story.* You intuitively knew that Rolf and all the Sharks were homos—straight guys don't dance in gazebos and back alleys. The great gay actors of the past (Rock Hudson, Montgomery Clift, Cary Grant, and James Dean) never played sissies on screen and were forever chasing skirts (except in their own bedrooms).

As a young adult, I finally found gay role models but at a different kind of show—dog shows! My gay role models were show-dog breeders, exhibitors, groomers, and judges. These men were passionate about raising dogs, showing dogs, and breeding dogs, and they were all involved in long-term gay relationships. The first couples I knew who were in twenty-year male/male relationships were active in Cocker Spaniels, Japanese Chins, Boxers, and Chow Chows. I also understood from these men that their dogs, their kennels of dogs, their many generations of champions, represented their *children.* This was family. They shared their homes with their "kids," and in many cases, the kids came first.

It's important to reiterate that these men *shared their homes* with their Cockers, Chins, Chows, and Boxers. They didn't just own dogs. Their dogs weren't possessions like Rolexes or Audis: these dogs were their children, expressions of the couples' devotion, love, and caring. No house is a home without a dog who's loved. For so many gay people, "family" comes at a price and is not taken for granted. The disconnect gays often feel between themselves and their parents and siblings weakens the family ties. When a newfound friend offers up his furry paw and his whole heart, some gay men discover "family" for the first time: at last a family that makes you feel at home.

Ten Life-Altering Doggy Lessons

1. How it feels to be the center of another's world
2. How it feels to have someone depend on you for everything
3. What unconditional love is
4. Why consistency pays off
5. That commitment doesn't hurt
6. Why the promise "to obey" can be a good thing
7. How it feels to wake up to a hairy beast who will never leave you for a younger man
8. What it's like to have a friend who never judges you
9. That dogs hang around longer than most lovers
10. The utter joy of a good bone

TOTO, DARLING!

While Judy Garland remains every gay man's iconic diva, it's her "little dog" who steals our hearts. Toto accompanies Dorothy on her journey to the Emerald City and proves that he has the brains, heart, and courage that her newfound misfit friends lack. Toto offers Dorothy unconditional love, and for many young gay people, Toto is their first hero.

For generations, gay youths have been mesmerized by the classic MGM musical *The Wizard of Oz*, which introduced Toto to the world. Theories abound as to why gays relate to the fantastical land of ne'er-do-wells that exists "Over the Rainbow." Invariably, life in the proverbial closet is shades of gray, and the world doesn't shimmer with Technicolor until the door is removed from its hinges. Essays and full-length books examining the spiritual, Zen Buddhist, Freudian, Jungian, and politico-anthropological interpretations of the movie analyze its appeal to queer boys. As for Toto, L. Frank Baum, author of the original Oz books, says that he is the only thing that brings Dorothy joy. Gay boys fall in love with Judy's little dog and the unconditional relationship the two share.

As gay men mature and discover that Judy traded in her little dog and the "Rainbow" to sing desperate torch songs, flipped the Scarecrow for three gay husbands, and swapped her "no place like home" for any shack with a good man, Judy outqueers Toto for days. Gay men, even some young ones, continue to regard Judy as the "Queen of Queens," and her place in gay history is secure. After a grieving drag queen snapped her heel on the night of Judy's funeral in June 1969, the historical gay riots at the Stonewall Inn in Greenwich Village broke out, forever immortalizing Judy's sainthood.

Over the years, Toto's breed has been a matter of much discussion. Jan Grebe, a scholar of all things Toto, shares her take on Judy's basket pooch:

> The very first of the L. Frank Baum Oz books was *The Wonderful Wizard of Oz*, published in 1900 and illustrated by W. W. Denslow. In that book, there was a dog named Toto who was described in this way: "a little black dog, with long, silky hair and small black eyes that twinkled

merrily on either side of his funny, wee nose." Although his breed was not specified, Denslow drew him to look kind of like a Cairn Terrier or maybe a Scottie . . . *In The Road to Oz* (1909), artist John R. Neill drew Toto as a kind of a rangy French Bulldog. . . . In subsequent books of the series, he came to be drawn as more and more terrier-like in appearance.

Grebe believes that Neill owned a Frenchie, and given the breed's popularity in the early twentieth century, it's very likely that he used his own dog as the model for his first Toto drawings.

In real life, the Toto in the movie was played by a Cairn Terrier named Terry, owned by Hollywood animal trainer Carl Spitz. In fact, Toto was a drag artist, a bitch portraying a male dog. She received $125 per week, an extremely high salary for a drag diva in 1939, so in her own way Toto did her part to further the LGBT movement.

CHOOSING A CANINE PARTNER

Let's explore all of the reasons that a gay man needs a dog. Dogs can be an instant cure for loneliness. This adorable button-nosed creature thinks of you as the center of his universe, and you feel needed and wanted.

Every gay man likes to feel wanted, even if it's just for a scratch on the head or a toss of a Frisbee. As companions, dogs provide the perfect complements to their owners. A dog makes an ideal walking or running mate, cheerfully keeping up with your pace and always ready to go whenever he sees you pick up his rainbow leash. Likewise, a dog is happy to sit by your side as you catch up on *Vanity Fair* or the evening news. He's also happy to climb into bed and take a midday nap.

Dogs can allay a gay man's fears of rejection, responsibility, and commitment. A dog can open up your world with his unrestrained affection and dependence. Author Stephen McCauley sums up a gay man's initial reluctance to own a dog as "alternating between fearing slobbering dependence upon (you) and the possibility that the dog might not like (you)." Dogs are excellent judges of character and have other traits that gay men envy, including their ability to forgive instantly, to accept an apology, and to never be spiteful on your silk pillowcase. Gay men have got to start somewhere, so why not take the chance and commit to a four-legged partner?

For some guys, dogs are actually *better*—think about all the ways dogs are superior to a boyfriend:

- Dogs are far more tolerant of your shortcomings and your insecurities.
- Dogs actually listen to you when you speak.
- Dogs are all about PDA.
- Dogs don't insist on exclusivity: threesomes in the park would be every dog's idea of the perfect Saturday outing.
- Dogs are easy to get along with and don't bitch about your spending too much money at Pottery Barn or Saks.
- Dogs don't question you when you bring home the sales boy from Pottery Barn or Saks.
- Dogs freely admit that they are nosy and love gossip, and they rarely repeat it.
- Dogs don't complain when you opt for dinner at home, even if it's only leftovers.
- Dogs don't insist on an explanation when you come home late or stay out all night.
- Dogs don't compare you with their previous bedmates.
- Dogs actually enjoy being used.

Finally, the best reason a dog outclasses a boyfriend is summed up in a recent Paul Simon lyric: your dog's still "gonna love ya when your looks are gone." Most guys in man-hunting mode slim themselves down to Whippet conformation. You can bet your buff new boyfriend's going to run when your Bullmastiff ass starts to rear its ugly cheeks again.

MAN MAGNET

Another vital role of the dog for the single gay man is that of man magnet. Your future husband absolutely can't resist checking out the well-muscled buttocks and tucked-up abs of your flashy Boxer, with his chiseled good looks and aristocratic air. Nothing turns the head of a gay man faster than a fabulous puppy being walked by his equally fabulous owner. When you find the perfect canine partner to match your lifestyle and personality, one who is aesthetically and physically your ideal, the two of you will be impossible to ignore.

Consider how much easier it is to meet guys in the Castro when you're walking a Golden Retriever puppy. The likelihood of gay men introducing themselves to you, actually speaking to you and looking you in the eye—not just covertly coveting your Armani-stamped ass—is increased by six times if you're walking a Golden puppy; it is increased by ten times if you're walking a pair of French Bulldog puppies! Hell, even straight guys will go out of their way to strike up a conversation. A man walking a dog is more approachable, and the dog at the end of the lavender leash tells volumes about your taste, lifestyle, and preferences.

Remember that dogs like to be used, whether it's for jogging, biking, sharing dinners at home, or luring humpy bad boys into your lair. Dogs are happily at your service, and soon others will be, too.

Admittedly, the kind of guy you're trying to attract affects the kind of dog you buy. If you're usually on the prowl for strong daddy types or handsome homeboys, the Bichon Frisé is not going to do it. You'll need a real man's dog. If you're attracted to the more sensitive guy or the intellectual Homemaker type, a Rottweiler will scare this fairy back up his tree. However, if you're just a mess and need someone to take care of you, then your choice of breed isn't going to matter all that much. You can start at the pound.

If your chosen canine buddy is going to be your sex lure, you ought to start hitting the pavement right away. Sauntering through Piedmont Park, down Christopher Street, or around Dupont Circle is a great way to start your pup's social life and improve your own. For suburban types, it's time to make a pilgrimage to Homo Depot or a major garden center. You can walk the puppy around the store entrance and meet every hot guy picking up a new drill bit or a flat of pansies. (The latter may go home with one more pansy than he paid for.) Socializing a puppy outside a major shopping center is not cruising (technically), but it's just as much fun and serves your needs and the puppy's, too. Keep in mind that puppies have twice the appeal of adult dogs, whether it's their puppy smell, round heads, big eyes, big feet, or soft fur. Even the toughest straight (-acting) guy says, "Ahh," when he sees a baby Boxer or a long-eared Basset—and you're halfway home.

Good Reasons *Not* to Get a Dog

- You love puppies and can't resist the smell
- Your new boyfriend really loves dogs, but you're indifferent, allergic, or desperate
- You can't find a good boyfriend to take up your free time
- You want to trap a man
- You think a dog will complement your decor
- You can afford a high-fashion pooch
- You sound smart when you pronounce rare breed names
- You can put a puppy on AmEx, but you can't charge a real baby
- You want to impress your friends with a cleverly named, show-quality, smartly dressed child substitute

A puppy on the end of your rainbow leash invites an admiring man into your personal space. A puppy instantly gives you something to talk about. How amazing that some scrumpy stranger is kneeling down in front of you to talk to and pet your furry and soft accomplice!

Now go slowly, and don't blow it.

Do not sound desperate or bitter. Do not profess your undying love for your Boxer puppy. Do not ask for the guy's number or for permission to sniff his treasure trail, too. Do not babble incessantly about the evils of designer dogs or the foibles of finding a suitable stud for your last champion bitch. Just enjoy the moment of sharing your soft little dog. You have something in common. Focus on the puppy, and let him cast his spell. Nothing you can say will be as effective as a rough puppy tongue on an unsuspecting chin. Just say, "Ahh."

Be forewarned: "man-magnet" canines have backfired in the past. This cannot be the deciding factor in adopting a dog. There is the very real possibility that your elegant English Setter companion or sunny Skye Terrier pal will be labeled baggage by your future ex-boyfriend. It may be fabulous Fendi baggage but baggage nonetheless. For centuries, dogs have been known to spoil booty calls. Caligula's forty mastiffs are said to have derailed a number of his sweatiest slumber parties. Some men don't like dogs. Some have never lived with dogs. Some have been traumatized by dogs. Some are indifferent, fearful, or allergic.

If you decide to buy a dog, make it a lasting commitment. You don't want to abandon your best friend for a spur-of-the-moment Cowboy with dander issues. That's no way to treat a creature who's enlightened you to the joys of unconditional love. Find a man who shares your enthusiasm for dogs. Thank heavens, there are leagues of them!

THE BOY WHO CRIED "WOOF!"

Are you ready for a dog? Owning a dog is a real long-term commitment. Most dogs will outlive your current boyfriend's good looks. Too often guys fall in love with the idea of being a dog owner but aren't prepared to sacrifice the time and energy to raise a puppy. Let's look at what's really involved in adopting and caring for a dog.

Choosing a Canine Partner

For many gay men, the first consideration is aesthetics. What look are you after? It's a matter of physique. It's physical. Is he attractive, handsome, well balanced, aristocratic, well muscled? Does he have a beautiful head? Can his dark brown eyes melt a bitch from forty yards?

Certainly, the most important consideration for gay men is size, and yes, this applies to the selection of a dog, too. How do you decide on the right size for you? From giants to dwarfs, the dog world has a size for everyone. The largest dogs in weight and height are giants such as the Mastiff, the Irish Wolfhound, and the Great Dane, dogs who can weigh upward of 200 pounds and stand as tall as thirty-six inches at the withers. At the Lilliputian end, we have the tiniest of breeds, such as the Yorkshire Terrier, the Maltese, and the Chihuahua, who can weigh one or two pounds and stand only a few inches high. The ideal size of a dog may be governed by your living space; however, the dog's activity level must be taken into consideration as well. Many city dwellers happily live with those giants who require only a bed on which to stretch their limbs until you come home from work or play.

The activity level of different breeds varies tremendously. Breeds that were devised to hunt or herd tend to be the most active. It would be difficult to house a Pointer or a Border Collie in your midtown apartment and not come home to a badly redecorated mess five days a week. Even an hour running through the park will not satiate these outdoorsy overachievers. There are many moderately active breeds that will suit the moderately active guy who wants to bike or to jog with a dog in tow. Less active breeds, such as the Pembroke Welsh Corgi and the Basset Hound,

Trio Sonata

Ever fantasize about taking home twins? It happens more often than you think. Many gay men adopt matching pairs of dogs for practical and aesthetic reasons. Consider adopting two Bulldogs and naming them "Howard" and "Robin" or two Chihuahuas and naming them "Mary-Kate" and "Ashley."

Many owners find that keeping two dogs is hardly more effort than keeping one. You can feed, walk, and socialize two dogs at the same time. Grooming salon, veterinarian, and day care visits require but a single appointment. The best advantage of having two dogs is the all-day company that the dogs provide for each other. Usually, opposite-sex pairs get along better, although same-sex pals can bond just as closely, depending on the breed.

City Girls, Guppies, and other urban guys who work full-time subscribe to the notion that twins waiting at home are better than one lonely pooch. A recent visit to the Castro revealed more boys walking pairs of dogs than individual dogs. Frenchies, Bulldogs, Westies, Aussies, and English Setters were among the braces we embraced. I even met an angelic Cali Boy with a trio of Cavaliers named "Sabrina," "Kelly," and "Jill." Heaven on earth.

make better candidates for smaller homes and gay men who don't belong to a gym.

The amount of coat that a dog has also plays a part in the selection process. Most breeds have double coats—a harder outer coat over the soft downlike undercoat that sheds seasonally *and* daily. Doggy down (the undercoat) can tumble under every piece of furniture in the house. If you are a fastidious Anal Perfectionist or an OCD cleaning dervish with a Dyson, then a Chow Chow or an Old English Sheepdog is not the companion for you. There are many breeds that have single coats, and these coats do not shed as much. The most famous example is the Poodle, but that fabulous girl does require monthly trips to the salon. Other parlor pooches include the Bichon Frisé, the Cocker Spaniel, the Shih Tzu, the Maltese, and the Lhasa Apso. Dogs with long coats require nearly daily grooming to keep them from tangling and matting, and the wirehaired dogs, such as the West Highland White Terrier, the Brussels Griffon, and the Wire Fox Terrier, require special care as well. Practically all of the terrier breeds require the right hand to keep their coats glistening and hard, the way they should be! Are you up to the task?

As the old saying goes, "A queen's home is his castle," and many such castles have graced the covers of major magazines such as *Better Homos and Gardens.* Surely the staff at MSLO has been welcomed into fabulous gay dwellings all over North America. For gays who are particularly attached to their belongings, dogs may pose a major inconvenience. If you envision yourself having a Nellie fit the first time your Pug piddles on your Persian carpet, then you may want to reconsider a puppy in the house (or consider puppy proofing your palace).

Time is a major part of the commitment to a companion, whether canine or human. Consider how much time you can devote to your four-legged pal before you select him. Certain breeds—like too many gay men—require a high level of maintenance. The dogs may require daily grooming time, hours of physical activity, special training, or just lots of attention to keep them occupied. If you truly think a dog would be a positive force for your life, no matter how busy you are, then you will make time for him. Just as gay men can find the time for constant coupling during the first months of a steamy new romance, these same love-starved men can find time to commit to the needs of a new puppy for the first few months. By the third month of puppy ownership, life settles down and the dog demands less of your time. Not unlike dating a trophy bartender or a Biscuit who Rollerblades.

This brings us to the discussion of temperament. Even if you find a dog who aesthetically pleases you, the dog may not behave the way you would like (not unlike the aforementioned Rollerblading blade). Some breeds are very independent and are content just to know you're home; others are clingier than a Twink on his last dime. You may love the look of the sleek Basenji or the glamorous Afghan Hound, but if you're craving cuddly attention in the evening hours, these dogs will not oblige. Every dog doesn't act like a needy Labrador Retriever or an over-caffeinated Border Collie. Temperaments range from the aloof and rather distant sighthound and Nordic dog types—such as the Basenji, the Afghan Hound, the Shiba Inu, and the Siberian Husky—to the sweet and happy-to-please herding dogs, such as the German Shepherd Dog and the Collie, to the feisty, independent terriers to the tail-wagging gay spaniels. In fact, each breed of dog has a different temperament, and surely there's a good-looking dog out there with a temperament that will make you wag your gay tail, too.

LOVE CONQUERS ALL

Gay men living with HIV/AIDS may be reluctant to adopt a dog for practical reasons as well as health considerations. However, people infected may lose friends, employment, and their health, so the advantages of a loving canine companion, offering that unique brand of no-strings-attached love, far outweigh the health risks. Psychologist Gary Bachman comments, "With the loss of lovers, friends, and family members, a dog can help fill this void. Dogs are also often taken to the homes of the ailing, hospitals, and hospices, where they are met with delight."

> "I can honestly say that at times these animals, my lifelines and my protectors, have saved my life just as profoundly, just as miraculously, as the medications I take every day."
>
> —Greg Louganis

Olympic Gold medalist Greg Louganis, who's lived with HIV for over a decade, wouldn't go a day without his canine family. In his book *For the Life of Your Dog* (1999), he puts it like this: "Dogs have always been important players in my life.

Sometimes I think I may even owe them my life. Living with HIV, I have come to know personally and intimately the exquisite power of the human/animal bond. I don't need scientific research studies to tell me that when you share a special relationship with animals—in my case dogs—your outlook improves, you enjoy a more fulfilling life,

and most significantly, you are better equipped to heal and to fight off disease." Louganis, as you may know, has bred and shown Great Danes for years.

A dog owned by a person with HIV/AIDS must remain in optimal health, with the assistance of a savvy veterinarian, and must be well trained so that he doesn't present problems to dog sitters, dog walkers, and friends who volunteer to help out. People living with AIDS can be more susceptible to zoonotic infections (those that can be passed from an animal to a person), although they're more likely to become sick from other people, food, water, and soil than from their own well-kept pets.

When selecting a dog, be certain that you know where he comes from. If you're rescuing a dog, have a veterinarian thoroughly examine him for parasites and possible illnesses. You're wiser adopting a puppy or adult dog from a breeder who can guarantee the environment and overall health of the animal. Choose a breed whose energy level, exercise, and space requirements match your own. Even if you're a Size Queen jonesing for a Dobie, you're better off with a dog that doesn't terrify your good-hearted dog sitters. A smaller dog with a good health record makes the best choice. Consider a Miniature Poodle, a Beagle, or almost any small terrier, such as the Westie or the Cairn.

Nurse Patti says: be sensible first and foremost. Keep your dog well groomed so that Princess doesn't bring home fleas, and keep his nails short. Don't let your dog sniff around in the grass or soil, and use gloves whenever picking up his droppings. No matter how cute he is, never let him French you.

ON THE COUCH
WITH GARY BACHMAN

Get comfy ladies, and take advantage of some free psychotherapy with our favorite New England psychologist and dog lover. Your session begins now:

From a developmental perspective, it is often at the onset of adolescence when many young men realize they want their sexual and affectional needs met by another man. Fearing parental disapproval and a lack of peer support, and seeing negative images in the media, they harbor a secret and often withdraw socially. As a way to self-soothe, a dog with its unconditional love can be a great source of comfort. This notion is underscored by a recent television ad for dog food whose slogan is, "There is nothing more real than a dog."

In my experience, many gay men are attracted to the flat-faced breeds such as the French Bulldog and Pug due to their undeniably humanlike faces. But there is certainly a breed for everyone, and owning a dog gives one a great sense of joy. The heartbreak comes when a dog dies, since we humans have much longer life spans. This loss is devastating to many.

Many gay men are childless, although some couples do adopt nowadays. For a couple desiring children but unable to have them, a dog often becomes their "child."

In psychology we have what is known as Attachment Theory. This, in brief, explains how the emotional bond between parents and children affects the bonds that form between adults in both romantic and other intimate relationships. Research has even shown that attachment occurs in other primates and dogs. So for many gay men, whether single or coupled, who have lost parental nurturance, it is not surprising that they choose a life shared with dogs.

When relationships end, this can be a difficult time. A pooch is perhaps the "best medicine." When a new man enters the picture, a dog can at first be quite possessive but more often than not acceptance is not far away.

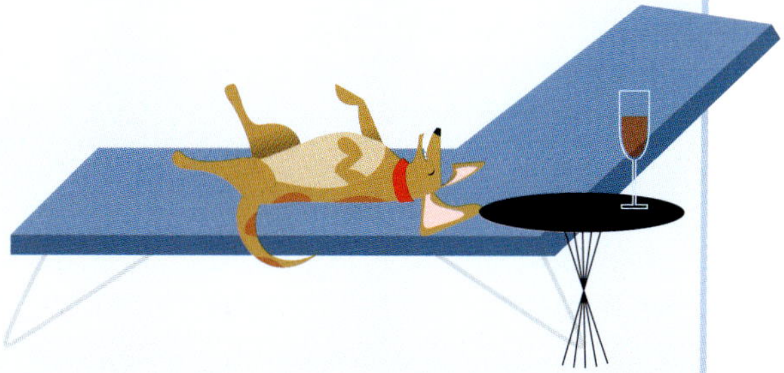

Sorry, our time is up for today.
See you next week!

A RAINBOW OF PURBRED DOGS

A ruby Cavalier, a burnt-sienna Boxer, a yellow Labrador, a grass-stained Maltese, a blue-merle Aussie, and a lavender Chinese Crested—a dog for every color of the rainbow!

Color should never be the deciding factor, but it can inspire and rouse our imaginations. Poodles alone come in seven colors and hundreds of hues, as do Lhasa Apsos, Shih Tzu, and Chow Chows. Just think: you can drink in a café-au-lait Poodle, a honey Lhasa, a cream Shih Tzu, or a cinnamon Chow. Delish!

The doggy menu is expansive, but fortunately it's organized by breed and group to help facilitate your selection. The American Kennel Club (AKC) divides its breeds of dog into seven groups: Sporting, Hound, Working, Terrier, Toy, Non-Sporting, and Herding. For the most part, these groups are based on the breeds' original and current purposes, such as hunting, guarding, hauling, herding, and killing vermin.

Before we begin our tour of the dog world, keep in mind that when you select a breed, you are making a major statement about yourself. You *decide* to own a Greyhound or a Brussels Griffon. Indecisive gay men, who often decide not to decide, should probably adopt a mutt or a mixed breed; that way, they can't go wrong. Most gay men, however, tend to know what type of dog they like, just as they know what kind of guy attracts them. Remember that in the dog world it's not *just* about size and physique; there are other considerations, too.

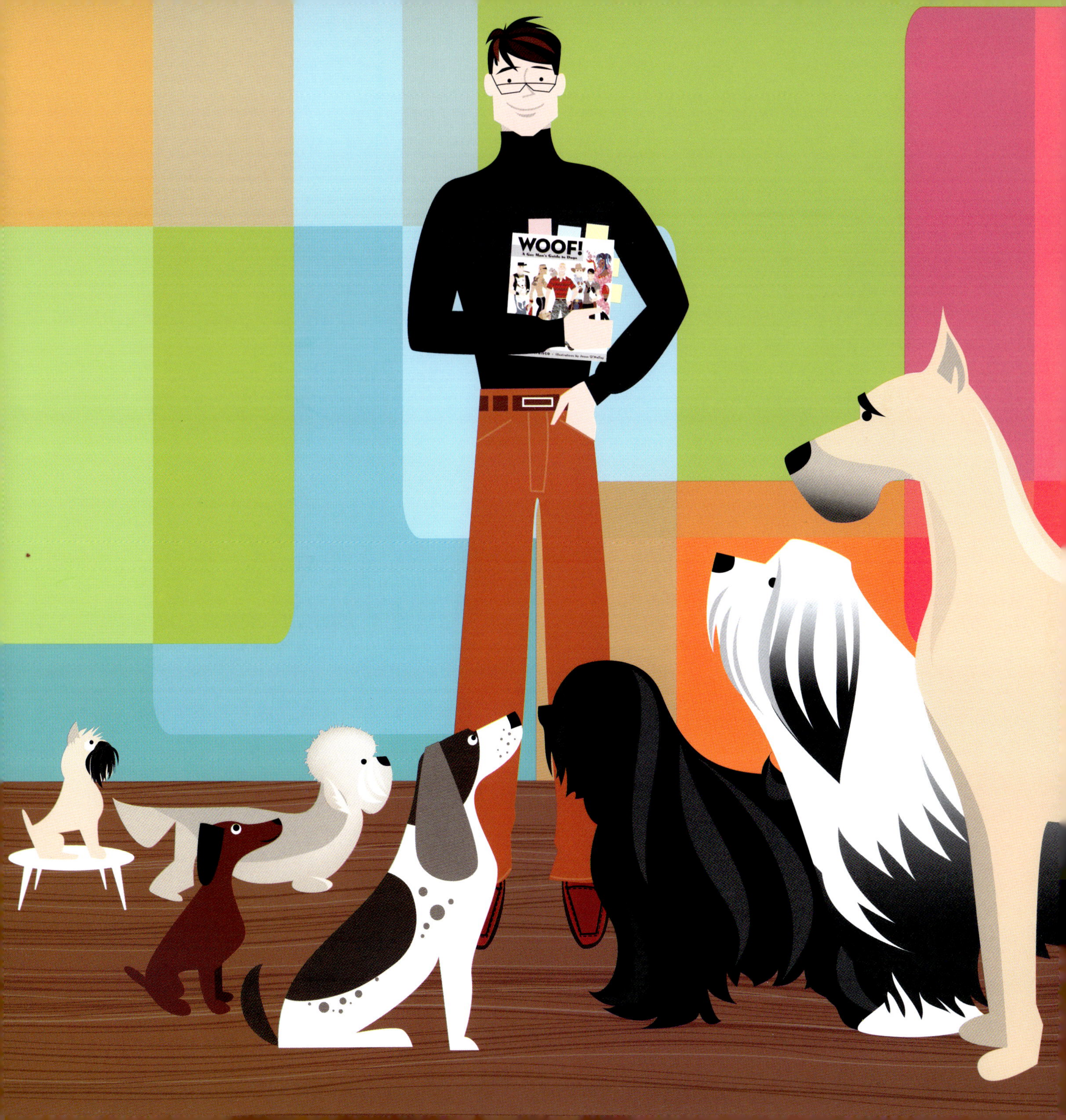
WOOF!
A Gay Man's Guide to Dogs

THE SPORTING GROUP

The Sporting Group contains the most macho of dog breeds: the hunters. We're talking about spaniels, pointers, setters, and retrievers. These dogs aren't hunting for chicken on the weekend. They're after real birds in the field, and they are often followed by rugged beer-swilling hunters in flannel, who might easily be mistaken for lesbians. Sporting dogs for the most part are incurably straight, even though some of these dogs (such as the Cocker Spaniel and the English Springer Spaniel) have fabulous coats. Every gay man has a soft spot for the flushing spaniels: How often can you use the word *cock* as a verb?!

The two most popular breeds in America are sporting dogs—the Labrador Retriever and the Golden Retriever—two dogs who are quintessential family companions. Handlers and breeders of some of the winningest Golden Retrievers in the country, Ken Matthews and Wayne Miller, tell us why Goldens are their best pals: "Goldens are like gay men themselves: the males are men's men, yet very cuddly . . . and furry. They're the best dogs for just having a buddy to hang out with and not bad for taking a walk with someone new. It kind of announces that you are lovable. We love Goldens because we're both very outdoorsy people. Everything we love to do revolves around the outdoors and the Pacific Northwest, where we live. We are both very spontaneous and so are the Goldens. We say, 'Want to try this?' and the Goldens always say, 'Sure!!' (A virtue in a great partner, too!)."

The pointing dogs, too, offer much appeal, especially the all-purpose Pointer, the solid rust-colored Vizsla, and the fully feathered and flecked English Setter. There's no mistaking that the Pointer is a dog who's ready to go, "his muscular body bespeaking both staying power and dash." Rugged and rigid gay men on both sides of the Mississippi love the Pointer for his loyalty and devotion. Hungary's golden boy, the Vizsla, rivals the Pointer in eagerness and devotion, and he's a true lover of a dog. Versatile and naturally brawny, Vizslas love to be active, involved, and fondled. Who can resist those adjectives in a roommate? The English Setter, one of three setters in the Sporting Group, is the eye candy of the trio, the most beautiful and aristocratic, and equally lovable. This is an elegant and graceful dog whose style is classic Ralph Lauren.

Among the sporting breeds, it's the spaniels that have flushed the most gay hearts, including the English Springer Spaniel, the Irish Water Spaniel, and the Cocker Spaniel. Cockers, of course! Here are Lloyd Alton and Bill Gorodner, longtime Cocker breeders, on their mouthwatering breed: "Cockers are livable and lovable and provide the incentive for nurturing that is at the heart of nearly every gay guy's existence. Cockers, when they love you, permeate your very soul and provide comfort in times of sorrow. They are active

Who You Calling "Sissy"?

Can a particular breed of dog make a person appear "gay"? The author understands the Q allure of the Poodle, and so do thousands of other gay men around the world. In a recently published article, top judge and Poodle authority Dr. Jacklyn Hungerland defends the "Integrity of Poodles" by saying, "Once a person has known a Poodle 'personally,' they are hooked into a lifetime of admiration and devotion, never again to refer to a Poodle as a 'sissy dog.'"

When has the always-tolerant, over-the-top Poodle ever complained about being called a sissy?! In fact, he hasn't; he revels in his bows and pom-poms and big hair. Well-known cat and dog breeder Dick Gebhardt poses this query: "If you saw John Wayne walking down the boulevard with a Toy Poodle, would he look femme to you?" The Duke could be wearing a feather boa and rhinestone earrings and still look butch. Thus, why blame a Poodle for your irreversible queerness? Alternatively, would a Drag Queen look butch walking a Kelpie or a Dingo through the Outback? (Probably not, especially if she's screaming, "That Dingo ate my baby!!")

Top breeder and judge Bo Bengtson doesn't believe that a dog breed necessarily has a gay allure. "The idea that your sexual preference might influence your choice of breed never really made much sense to me." Having been involved in the dog-show scene for more than four decades, Bo attributes "the much higher percentage of gay men involved in Poodles and the coated Toy and Non-Sporting breeds compared with Rottweilers, Cattle Dogs, or Staffordshire Bull Terriers" to tolerance and safety in numbers. He adds:

> Once a couple of charismatic and high-profile gay guys get involved in a particular breed, the interest among other gays spirals. Their friends get interested, and *their* friends also think this looks like fun, and before you know it you have a breed that's almost dominated by gays. . . . I don't think it's that gays are less likely to be interested in Terriers or Working dogs than others, just that some breeds and groups provide a more congenial and tolerant atmosphere than others. . . . It's refreshing when somebody breaks out of the box and provides an exception to the above. I know gay men who show Labrador Retrievers and German Shepherds, and I know perfectly straight family fathers who show Toy Poodles and Japanese Chins. A couple of gay friends who were getting a dog from the pound thought long and hard and then got a Foxhound.

Gay men with a Foxhound! Now, that *is* refreshing. As Dr. Hungerland observed, "Husbands and seasoned hunters have been known to sit on the kitchen floor feeding their Poodle puppies lobster from a can because they were worried about whether or not the pup was eating enough." Again, let's not blame the Poodle, but wives, if these aforementioned husbands are your own, don't let them go fishing on Brokeback Mountain without a rod and bait!

enough to be up to going anywhere or doing anything at any hour. The Cocker, as it has evolved, has gone from being a scraggly, plain, sporting companion to being a true glamour dog. Cockers provide an aesthetic sense of beauty in an almost unlimited array of colors and will love you unconditionally."

Top sporting-dog breeder Doug Johnson of Clussexx fame spells out the gay appeal of his beloved Sussex Spaniel: "The Sussex Spaniel would appeal to many aspects of gay life—he is easygoing and has lots of personality, a constant smile, and a massive well-toned body! The lovely golden liver color is exclusive to this breed. He is a rare find indeed . . . something the gays love . . . always putting a new spin on an old favorite. It's not just a spaniel, it's a Sussex Spaniel." Heaven help the lispy queen who falls in love with that quadruple-sibilant dog! *"Meet Thathy, my Thutheth Thpaniel."*

> "If the *s-e-x* in the name doesn't get you, consider this: Who wouldn't enjoy coming home to a golden boy with natural blonde highlights and a tail that never stops wagging?"
>
> —Doug Johnson, Clussexx Clumber and Sussex Spaniels

Doug also has much affection for his other short-legged spaniel, the Clumber Spaniel: "This white, broad-chested breed is solidly built with a keen nose for the better things in life. Described as the Elderly Gentleman's hunting companion, the Clumber would be perfect for outdoorsmen with plenty of time on their hands. Clumbers are slow, not ones to rush into things even if eager to please and happy with anyone. They are not early morning risers; they enjoy their breakfast in bed. Once only owned by the British royalty, and still currently bred by Princess Anne, fortunately the Clumber is now available to any queen."

THE HOUND GROUP

Not all members of the Hound Group hold equal allure for gay men. The dogs that hunt by scent (scenthounds) tend to be sloppy and slobbery, excessively vocal, and a little dim. (Those attributes describe half of the gay men in New Jersey, but I digress.) Nevertheless, there are a couple of exceptional scenthounds who have nosed up to gay men. Our hands-down favorite is the Dachshund, sometimes lovingly referred to as the Weiner Dog. Curiously, the Dachshund is one of the most popular choices for lesbians, a fact that would have pleased Dr. Freud to no end. The ever-popular Beagle, especially the irresistible thirteen-inch model, corners the market on cuteness and southern charm. The "gentle and pleading" expression of the Beagle's soft brown eyes could make the most unmovable gay man roll over and beg. The long and low Basset Hound and his tousled, wirehaired cousin the PBGV (Petit Basset Griffon Vendéen) also have many gay fans, and rightly so. The foxhound and coonhound breeds rarely find places in the gay world, as gay men are not allowed to own—no less wear!—camouflage clothing.

The sighthounds, the dogs that hunt by eye, are the runners in the family, those long-legged, elegant athletes that compete in dog racing, once known as the sport of queens. Sighthounds, therefore, hold more fascination for gay men, especially the very fabulous Afghan Hound, whose coat and regal bearing are flawlessly queer when presented properly. With a surprisingly large queer following, the Whippet attracts a lively field of gay men. Breeders and partners Randy Tincher and Johnnie Roe talk about this breed: "I think initially gay men are attracted to the beautiful, graceful curves of the Whippet silhouette. Their large, dark eyes and soft expression definitely draw you in. Whippets, however, aren't just living art. They are true athletes. Any doubts about that, just go to a lure-coursing event or watch when a squirrel happens into their yard. Some gay men might also be attracted to the Whippet personality: pure *DIVA*. Their agenda comes first. Their ideas are always best."

What the Whippet has to offer in his twenty inches, the Greyhound has to offer in ten more inches. Laura Thompson, author of *The Dogs,* describes her beloved Greyhounds as "slightly raffish, wonderfully old-style, worldly and shrewd and soft at heart," the perfect canine for a queen who's run the tracks and seen it all.

We cannot forget the Anna Karenina of the Hound Group, the breathtaking Borzoi, once known as the Russian Wolfhound. Canadian breeders Dr. John Reeve-Newson and Dr. Richard Meen paint us a truly fabulous portrait of the Borzoi:

> The gay appeal of the Borzoi is twofold: artistic and romantic. First the artistic sense: the beautiful lines of the breed, so graceful, sinuous, and harmonious. Slim and elegant (what most gay men are or would like to be), and in attitude slightly disdainful of the common. This is why the breed appealed to artists such as Erté and the art deco crowd. Second, the romantic history of the breed: being owned by the aristocracy of Russia and that appeal of the lost romance of prerevolutionary Russia, Nicholas and Alexandra, Tolstoy's *War and Peace*, the jewels of Fabergé, and the grandeur and beauty of that lost time; the Borzoi is in some ways really a living link to and symbol of that era and epoch. While our world today on the whole has lost style, glamour, and class, the Borzoi as a breed still has it. They are really the divas of the dog world: they still think that they are all grand dukes and duchesses and that the revolution never really happened.

Who would think that a lion-pinning hunting dog could arrest so many queer safari lovers?

Breeders Greg Castillo and David Bueno tell us why: "The Rhodesian Ridgeback is about as macho a dog as a gay guy can handle. Having a Ridgeback next to you will make even the most Nellie guy seem, well, less Brokeback. *Dirty Dancing*'s Patrick Swayze has Ridgebacks, but so does Jason Newstead [Metallica's former bass player], so there will be no stereotyping if you own one." (Aren't you glad they told you who Jason Newstead was! Lord knows your Opera Queen author had no clue. Pardon the interruption.) Our two wrangling Ridgeback breeders continue: "Ridgebacks also are neat and clean, which of course is a must. They don't fling slobber all over, which would require any gay man to place the dog in rescue. The downside is that there is no fussing with hairdos on the Ridgeback, leaving a gay guy with much too much time on his hands. Ridgebacks are thinkers; they do best when challenged to use their brains and are kept busy . . . more like Will and less like Jack."

SGM Seeks Companion of Mixed Heritage

Not every queen envisions himself with a purebred dog sharing his throne. Some gay men actually are attracted to mutts, mongrels, and mixed breeds. These same gays tend to date jobless bad boys, humpy hip-hoppers, and busty minxes from the wrong neighborhoods. And yet there's something endearing about dogs of the "Benji" type that a pedigreed dog cannot offer. Regardless of his heritage, a sweet, bright-eyed, waggy-tailed mongrel can make a delightful companion. Mutts are held in high esteem for their clean bills of health, which some people label hybrid vigor, as well as their friendly personalities and adaptability. A virtue encompassed by the sassy mixed-breed dog is one that every queer guy seeks in his companion: unencumbered versatility.

Like the Borzoi, the Saluki has a mystical allure that goes back to biblical times in Persia and Arabia. While gay tours of the Saluki's homeland promise little more than imprisonment, the breed has cast its spell on the gay sect that appreciates a beautiful, dignified dog who requires minimal pampering and has the force and flair to down a gazelle.

Finally, don't forget that tall, hairy Scotsman who makes all of our kilts a little tighter: the Scottish Deerhound. Although he's not flashy or glamorous, this rugged, rough-haired greyhound has been celebrated by painters, poets, and sculptors for centuries (and more recently stacked up lavender points for his cameo with Meryl Streep in *Out of Africa*).

THE WORKING GROUP

The Working Group is the hero club, and what gay man doesn't love heroes? Whether it's a buff war hero, Wonder Woman, or a shirtless Tom Welling playing Clark Kent, gay men live for hero worship. Among the courageous canines in this group are the St. Bernard, the Newfoundland, the Siberian Husky, the Great Dane, the Rottweiler, the Giant Schnauzer, the Doberman Pinscher, and the Boxer. These are tough, hardworking dogs who will attract equally hard men, if that's what you're aiming for (and who isn't?).

For unmistakable gay allure, the Boxer cuts an imposing silhouette. Recognized the world over as the top Boxer breeder in America, Rick Tomita shares his love of the breed: "The Boxer is a strapping athlete, muscular yet elegant, stylish, and proud. For a gay man who loves a handsome, well-proportioned companion with chiseled features, a broad chest, and clean, hard muscles, the Boxer cannot disappoint. Boxers love to kiss but are discreet and refined in public."

Another brawny German player makes the team—there is nothing like a Dane! For gay men seeking size for size's sake, and all the attention they can handle, the Great Dane earns his title of the Apollo of Dogs. (In Greek mythology, of course, Apollo is Zeus's gay son, the one interested in music, poetry, and archery.) Danes should be more than just large: they must be balanced, courageous, powerful, and friendly.

The Siberian Husky and the Samoyed qualify as enduring working dogs and flawless companion animals, both breeds having spent centuries by man's side, driving, droving, and dreaming. The Husky is a true blue-eyed wonder, a tireless rescuer, and an everyday hero. The Sammy's disarming smile, natural beauty, and fluffy white teddy bear coat will make mush of any man with a sweet tooth for eye candy.

THE TERRIER GROUP

The Terrier Group would seem an unlikely category to attract gay men, and yet the allure of these intense, dapper dogs cannot be denied. This is the only group bred to kill: terriers are the exterminators of the dog world and rid the countryside of rats, foxes, and badgers (Oh, my!). Nowadays, we have burly straight men and soon-to-be-legal immigrants to handle these tasks so we don't have to worry about our Scottish Terrier's soiling his fabulous coat. The terriers also are known for having the biggest, strongest teeth in the dog world, an ironic fact when you consider that most of these breeds were developed in England. (Perhaps the toothy Prince William was a Westie in a former life!) Despite the proclivity of these dogs to bite rats—not a talent welcome at any dinner party I've hosted—the terriers are stylish in their wiry coats and are unbeatable as show dogs. The terriers have won more Best in Show awards than any other group: in fact, terriers have swept the Westminster Kennel Club Dog Show at almost 50 percent of the shows.

High on many guys' lists is the Cairn Terrier, given the Toto factor, and what longtime Cairn lover Tom Stark refers to as the breed's

> "The Scottish Terrier is similar to Dorothy's dog but has more class and is very savvy about street life."
>
> –Thom Parrotti

"stubborn, independent, and full of love" demeanor. The West Highland White Terrier, with its crisp, pure-white coat and perfectly sculpted head, also turns many gay men's heads. Breeder and judge Bill Ferrara says: "The Westie is the most loving dog I have ever owned, and his affection is given to everyone, human as well as animal. They really are masculine as well as hardy and truly loyal. My dogs are always happy, with their tails up and wagging, and they make me laugh most of the time. What can one say but that I truly love them and would never want to be without them."

Two other terriers that fulfill a gay man's desire for lots of spunk, great hair, and real fire are the Miniature Schnauzer and the Scottish Terrier. Both are no-nonsense utilitarian canines who have morphed into spirited, somewhat obedient, companions. Like most terriers, the Mini and the Scottie require trips to the salon to keep looking sharp. Scottie breeder Thom Parrotti defends his rugged little terrier as a premium choice for the rainbow set: "I could not think of a better dog for a gay man! The Scottish Terrier portrays a sense of style, even if his owner has none. Ralph Lauren wouldn't have a mutt in his ads: he chose the epitome of style, the Scottish Terrier."

Don Emslie and Tim Doxtater, Miniature Schnauzer breeders and exhibitors, brag about their breed of choice. "The Miniature Schnauzer is a great breed for guys—he's sturdy and has marathon endurance! He is a small dog with a big-dog attitude. Nonshedding and low in doggy odor, a properly trimmed Mini is a tidy picture, which appeals to the neat individual. He can be somewhat snobbish with people whom he does not know, but he's extremely devoted to his owner and people he's met. The Miniature Schnauzer is tailored enough to suit the fussiest queen and yet butch enough to be seen with Mr. Macho."

Sealyham Terriers, a bit more easygoing although no less determined than the Scottie or Mini, also make attractive pets and have sensational wiry white coats. Two other lesser known terrier breeds with untapped mainstream gay appeal include the Dandie Dinmont Terrier and the Skye Terrier. Successful Dandie breeders and exhibitors Dick Yoho and Steve Houser endorse their breed: "There is no better breed to own than Dandies. They are different in that they do not leave hair all over you or your home. They do not bark all the time, except when visitors come to call (to see them, of course). Dandies seem to have a sense of humor and have forgotten more than some people pretend to know. They attract attention to themselves and their owners, especially good-looking men! They certainly know how to win you over."

The Dandie Dinmont Terrier, in his pepper- or mustard-colored coat, ranks high in accumulated lavender points. Gay men adore the Dandie's uniqueness: his cotton candy topknot, his Clara Bow eyes, and his diva-may-care attitude. Although the Dandie may be easygoing and affectionate on the outside, he has the bold confidence of a well-endowed weekend warrior.

Breeders Dr. John Reeve-Newson and Dr. Richard Meen count themselves among the zealous devotees of the "rare and unusual" Skye Terrier breed: "Their Scottish character, loyalty, devotion, independence, and fierceness may also appeal to those people who have the same traits as the Skye itself. A Skye does not back down from any situation, or anybody for that matter. They are not called 'land sharks' without good reason. To handle and deal with a Skye takes a very special person, and most pet owners would find the Skye attitude hard to deal with."

THE TOY GROUP

The Toy Group collects the beautiful ones: tiny, ornamental, portable canines with Hollywood-size egos and grand diva attitudes. These low and mighty mites also live longer than your last six "relationships" combined. Just as no gay home is complete without a live-in pool boy, no gay home is complete without a toy dog! A Pekingese should be required furniture in every gay household. (You know that Pekingese were bred by eunuchs in Chinese castles. Have you ever met a butch eunuch?) There should be a federal law stating that any gay man who does not own at least one toy breed will have his gay card revoked by the government. The coated wonders in this group include the peerless Toy Poodle, the silky white Maltese, the childlike Shih Tzu, the perfect pocket pup

Frenchies in Domestic Diva Paradise

The author is delighted to invite breeder Suzanne Orban-Stagle Readmond of JustUs French Bulldogs to share her take on . . .

> Gay men and Frenchies! A match made in heaven—with a little help from me! Both are artistic, enchanting, and fun to be around. Gay men truly are most caring of their dogs, and I love to see the dressing of the Frenchies à la gay! Only one thing is better for my Frenchies than having two dads: that is to live in the home of Martha Stewart, who now has *two* of my Frenchies . . . one named Francesca and the other named Sharkey (after her editorial director, Kevin Sharkey). Martha *dotes* on her little girl Frenchies, and they are always appropriately attired while tooling around with their very, very famous Mom.

known as the Yorkshire Terrier, the effervescent Pomeranian, and the waddling Pekingese—all top-ten gay dog breeds.

Gay men needn't be put off by these gayest of canines. On the contrary, a tiny Maltese or Toy Fox Terrier won't make you look any queerer than your bangles, crisp T-shirt, or Gucci shades. Toy dog experts, judges, breeders, and partners for fifty years, Richard Gebhardt and John Bannon pose this "queery": "Why do heterosexual and gay men seem to shy away from cats and toy breeds of dogs? We never thought about it, as our records show, having owned and bred many toy breeds, especially the charming, catlike Japanese Chin. Many men feel toy breeds are too feminine and will create the wrong impression of their masculinity. We feel it's the opposite: the dog doesn't make you look feminine unless you are. The most important thing is to be secure in who you are."

There's no doubt that Chihuahua breeders Billy Miller and Kenny Saenz are secure about their breed and their manhoods: "The Chihuahua is the world's smallest breed . . . and about the only thing that is the 'smallest' that a gay man would brag about owning!" When it comes to the tiniest of the tiny, the ubiquitous Chihuahua is indeed the king of the toy box.

The Toy Group can boast having a complete cast of gay breeds, every one of them unique and fabulous in its own right. There are the elegant and brilliant butterfly-eared Papillon, the sweet and lovely Japanese Chin, the gay-stepping Italian Greyhound, the regal Miniature Pinscher, and two wiry comic fellows, the Brussels Griffon and the Affenpinscher. Breeder, author, and exhibitor Jerome Cushman has lived with Affenpinschers for many years; his analysis of the breed and recipe for queer life with an Affen are a hoot: "The Affenpinscher is a *fabulous* dog for a gay household. If you get one, you will never live without one and they generally live from twelve to sixteen years. The Affen is a quixotic little charmer who will make you laugh and will adapt easily to most situations. He is small enough to live comfortably in an apartment and to easily be carried around; he loves to travel with you but also adores entertaining at home. Affens can be drama queens but are a delight to live with and will love you more than anything or anybody. Mine tend to enjoy a Rob Roy with a cherry."

As is well known, gay men are especially fond of naked things: in this case, the Chinese Crested, the hairless phenomenon bred by Gypsy Rose Lee.

Maple leaf transplant to the Land of Redwoods, Allan Reznik, one of the Cavalier royals, shares this about his up-and-coming toy breed: "Cavalier King Charles Spaniels are soft, mellow, totally huggable, and want nothing more than to sit in your lap and snuggle forever. Portable enough to tuck under your seat on a plane, they will live happily in the smallest apartment, yet are energetic enough to jog with you, swim, and camp if you're the outdoorsy type. He's happy to be a dog, and walk rather than being carried, but he's too smart to refuse pampering if it's offered."

Breeders and eloquent authors Bill Gorodner and Lloyd Alton have shared their lives for five decades and credit their love of both Cockers and Pugs for their longevity. Their fondness for the Pug is unmistakable: "The Pug is droll, upbeat, and a true sybarite at heart and blends perfectly with a gay guy's quest for joy and creature comforts. From the late Duchess of Windsor to Lena Horne, Pugs have filled the bill as bosom buddies. Their comedic antics can raise the gay spirit from any of life's downers. The real thing, a Pug, whether in flashy fawn or basic black, is a perfect addition for a happy gay life."

THE NON-SPORTING GROUP

In the group that the AKC labels Non-Sporting, we naturally find many of the gayest of all breeds. The Poodle, the Bichon Frisé, the French Bulldog, and the Lhasa Apso are among the top-ten gay breeds; other Non-Sporting faves include the Shiba Inu, the Tibetan Terrier, the Löwchen, the Bulldog, the Tibetan Spaniel, and the Chow Chow. The Non-Sporting dogs are, by definition, misfits—they don't fit into any other group and no longer perform their original functions. Perhaps this explains why gay men are so fond of these unusual breeds.

The author has owned Shibas for the past sixteen years, and I can attest to the fact that a dog doesn't get any gayer than a Shiba! It's all drama, pleasure seeking, and attitude. Shibas are natural beauties, easy on the eyes; they are full of themselves, never burning with the desire to please you. Shibas are thoughtful and well meaning, which is rarely true of gay boys with tails as eye catching as the Shiba's.

Gay Icons and Their Dogs

Edward Albee............Irish Wolfhound
Bill Blass............Golden Retriever
Orlando Bloom............Sloughi/hound mix
Marlon Brando............Mastiff
Truman Capote............Bulldog
Oleg Cassini............Shih Tzu
Jake Gyllenhaal............Puggle/Shepherd mix
Elton John............Cocker/Shepherd/Rottweiler
Greg Louganis............Great Dane
Barry Manilow............Basset Hound
Ricky Martin............Golden Retriever
Michelangelo............Pomeranian
Brad Pitt............Weimaraner
Jason Priestley............French Bulldog
Yves St. Laurent............Boston Terrier/Frenchie
Rick Springfield............Bull Terrier/Great Dane
Sting............Irish Wolfhound
Justin Timberlake............Yorkshire Terrier
Rudolph Valentino............Pug

Although the Chow Chow's scowling expression, breathtaking lordliness, and long list of famous owners make fashionable gay men take notice, it is the breed's kind, approachable nature that should be the Chow's calling card. The Chow Chow standard refers to the breed as "a masterpiece of beauty, dignity and naturalism." Perhaps Georgia O'Keefe, an avid Chow lover, found the Chow too perfect to render on canvas. We are none the poorer, as we have lifelong Chow lover, breeder, author, and judge Dr. Samuel Draper to paint the Chow for us as only he can: "The most noble, magnificent and serene of all dogs, the Chow Chow brings to mind two distinct season images that would have inspired the canvases of Vermeer and van Gogh, artists of light and dark. The October Chow, in a profuse, offstanding coat of scarlet or noontime yellow, with a giant chrysanthemum head, instills in us an 'autumnal afternoon filled with bright sunlight.' And the December Chow, shades of light to dark blue, or a deep midnight black, a few snowflakes resting on his giant head, brings to mind a 'frosty winter night in sparkling moonlight.' "

Like the Lhasa Apso from Tibet, the Tibetan Terrier is a walking hairdo, irresistible to artists, hairstylists, and other creative types. The Tibetan Terrier's profuse long coat, which can be straight or wavy, enshrines a hardy, affectionate dog. Gay men around the globe have excelled at breeding and exhibiting TTs, transforming them from austere Dalai Lamas to bouncy Dolly Partons.

> "And, remember, if you're only a princess, the Pembroke Welsh Corgi will still love you like a queen."
>
> —Bill Shelton and Steve Leyerly, Coventry Pembrokes

THE HERDING GROUP

Once a part of the Working Group, the Herding Group pens the sheepdogs, including two famous hero dogs—the German Shepherd Dog and the Collie—both movie stars and therefore gay faves! All in all, the Herding Group has a number of terrific breeds to which gay men have flocked, including the dreadlocked Puli, every hairdresser's fantasy dog; the shaggy, easygoing Old English Sheepdog, the well-mannered TV star who didn't eat the daisies; the Australian Shepherd, a beauty among heel-biting canines; and the lovable Shetland Sheepdog, who even allows his straight friends to call him Sheltie. The dog who's deemed the smartest of all breeds, the Border Collie, is one of the most recognizable and accomplished Herding Group dogs. Even more popular with corn-fed Farm Boys is the boisterous, fun-loving Bearded Collie; like the boys from *OK!* the Beardie is "natural and unspoiled."

The two Welsh Corgi breeds are little dynamos with great personalities and no Napoleon complexes. Prominent Pembroke Welsh Corgi breeders and exhibitors Bill Shelton and Steve Leyerly usher us into the enchanted land of the dwarf from Pembrokeshire: "On numerous occasions, when out and about with our throng of Corgis, my partner Steve and I inevitably encounter someone running across a parking lot or field toward us, exclaiming, 'These are the Queen's dogs, aren't they?' We, of course, can only smile and reply, 'And *are* they.' " The advice of these breeders is simple: a Corgi can out you, whether you're a hardcore fairy or still a twixter.

Speaking fairies, let's return to Wales: "The Pembroke Welsh Corgi's history is deep rooted: the romantic tales the Welsh have passed on for centuries are vast. Chronicled with regularity is one particular legend that the Corgi was a gift from the fairies. The 'wee folk' of Wales used the Corgi either to pull their carriages or as fairy steeds in and about the forests." (Should any fairy doubt this, present-day Corgis still bear the mark over their shoulders of the little saddles used by their fairy riders.) "The Pembroke is a more than versatile buddy, which lends him to various home situations. Never let his twenty-seven pounds deter you from thinking he is a small dog, incapable of being athletic and thinking *big*. Be assured that the Pembie will never let you forget. Pembrokes prefer to be active but are always ready to spend a quiet evening with their best friends. Count on them being people magnets; don't be surprised to meet other lifelong companions through them."

As popular as many of the herding breeds are, gay men have historically avoided certain rugged, irrepressibly butch butcher dogs such as the Bouvier des Flandres as well as the raucous

Gay Divas and Their Dogs

Cindy Adams	Yorkshire Terrier
Lauren Bacall	Cavalier/Papillon
Tallulah Bankhead	Pekingese
Barbie	Afghan Hound
Brigitte Bardot	Irish Setter
Betty Buckley	Shih Tzu
Maria Callas	Poodle
Coco Chanel	Cavalier
Cher	Akita
Joan Crawford	Dachshund/Toy Poodle
Bette Davis	Scottish Terrier/Bichon Frisé
Doris Day	Collie
Debbie Harry	Japanese Chin/Pug
Sonja Henie	Boxer
Audrey Hepburn	Yorkie/Jack Russell
Katherine Hepburn	Cocker/Poodle
Grace Kelly	Poodle/Rhodesian Ridgeback
Jacqueline Kennedy	German Shepherd
Jeanette MacDonald	Old English Sheepdog
Madonna	Chihuahua/Maltese
Ann-Margaret	Pug
Bette Midler	Jack Russell Terrier
Liza Minnelli	Cairn Terrier
Marilyn Monroe	Bolognese/Basset Hound
Olivia Newton John	Great Dane/Irish Setter
Dorothy Parker	Dandie Dinmont Terrier
Bernadette Peters	American Pit Bull Terrier
Beverly Sills	Yorkshire Terrier
Martha Stewart	Chow Chow/French Bulldog
Barbra Streisand	Bichon Frisé
Mary Tyler Moore	Golden Retriever/Poodle
Elizabeth Taylor	Maltese/Shih Tzu
Deborah Voigt	Yorkshire Terrier

nipper known as the Australian Cattle Dog, even though the latter appeared briefly in *Brokeback Mountain.* If you are attracted to these breeds, Cowboy, you're in for a hard ride, so saddle up good and tight.

THE TEN GAYEST DOG BREEDS

Now let's look at our poll and see which breeds offer the most gay appeal. All of these breeds are glamorous, fabulous, and potentially over the top. These are the gayest dogs on the planet, and any hot, well-groomed guy walking one of these dogs is automatically suspect and therefore fair game. A word of caution: you can never be 100 percent certain that hunky male owners of any of these breeds are definitely "family," so cruise at your own risk. If, by chance, the owner is wearing beaded clogs and is carrying a pin brush and bottle of conditioner, pounce!

Poodles. Any size, any color, any day. Nobody can deny that magnetic queer allure of this perennially popular breed. It is the only breed whose main function today is to symbolize "fabulous"—it's Liberace with pom-poms! It is the world's greatest show dog, and by virtue of its superior air, supercanine intelligence, and BIG hair, the Poodle attracts an army of homos armed with thousands of brushes, blow dryers, and rubber bands. Plus a tanker of shampoo and conditioner. A genius with a pin brush, Frank Sabella, one of the most famous Poodle handlers in the world, was attracted to this exciting breed because of its grace, athleticism, and style. Trained as a classical ballet dancer, Sabella used his natural talent and grace to transform the Standard Poodles he groomed and handled into Best in Show winners, including the top prize at Westminster Kennel Club in 1973. Author, handler, and judge Patricia Trotter believes that the Poodle breed is a natural fit for gay men with attitude. "Let's face it: the gay world is 'poodley' in temperament; it's that outgoing aspect of the gay world that we love. Poodles are for the beautiful people—that sense of 'self' will always link the gay world and the Poodle."

Yorkshire Terrier. As the most popular toy dog in most American cities, the Yorkie undoubtedly has his share of gay appeal. The Yorkshire Terrier's story, as told by George Bernard Shaw, is one of transformation: a common British working-class dog evolves into a glamorous show dog through the magic of gay men with combs. Today's Yorkie is five pounds of blue hair and attitude that lives for luxury alone.

Shih Tzu. Like the ancient Asian drag queens who invented this breed back in the days of the Tang Dynasty and the Byzantine Empire, the Shih Tzu reclines on rice mats with hair as high as an elephant's eye. Could a straight man have conceived of that hairdo? The Shih Tzu historically was a palace pet and today is the choice of queens in both hemispheres.

The 10 Gayest Dog Breeds

Bichon Frisé. When have gay men ever been able to resist Italian sailors? The Bichon is said to have accompanied a band of Italian sailors from the Far East, thus proving that the Bichon's appeal to fags traces back centuries! Like the Poodle, the Bichon Frisé requires sculpting to look like a proper gay icon and has had a large following since it *arrived* on the American scene in the 1970s. Bichon pioneer Rick Beauchamp describes the breed as follows: "A French powderpuff in Dr. Dentons with personality plus—what self-respecting gay man could resist? Bichons love the world; no beast or (more important) man is a stranger. A breed that's rugged enough to accompany you on a mountain hike and eye-catching enough to help you along on those late evening 'constitutionals' down the boulevard—almost any place Mr. Right might happen along. And in the end, if the Bichon is good enough for Ms. Streisand, who are we to argue?"

Breeders Tray Pittman and Paul Flores hasten to add: "We love the Bichon Frisé because they exist for one purpose: to make their family happy! They are entertaining and delightful. Walking the streets of Europe and surviving both World Wars, the devil-may-care Bichons are good at tricks and still give crisp fashioned trim. It's easy to see why they're so appealing."

Maltese. In the days of Caligula's infamous White Parties, the Maltese was the "toy" in demand, imported from one of the world's centers of culture. They brought elite society pleasure and joy, and they were as expensive as "a herd of Roman cattle." That's one way to meet rugged Roman rancheros. A companion only for the refined set, the Maltese is the gentlest, most affectionate, and most playful of all silky dogs.

French Bulldog. In Victorian times, the breed was a runway fashion accessory, popular with the feminine set. Today the Frenchie is the Porsche of purebred dogs: he costs nearly as much but is always in "park." Like Noel Coward, this center-stage French/English entertainer possesses a true "talent to amuse"; he also doesn't mind dressing up in lace and frills and sharing a spot of tea with his dad. The Frenchie's gay royal connections lead us to the very doable Crown Prince Felix Yusupov, who shot Rasputin for fondling one of his Frenchie figurines. As breeder Gary Bachman shares, "French Bulldogs were bred for companionship and are little clowns with tons of personality. They seem to believe they are, as one breeder stated, little people dressed up in dog suits. An urban legend purports that the Frenchie was the companion of many of the 'ladies of the night' in Paris during the early twentieth century. Their antics made them so popular that they quickly became the darlings of the upper class. . . . When it comes to attention-getting, no breed matches the Frenchie."

Pekingese. A living tribute to masculine beauty, the Pekingese was esteemed as the Lion

Dog of China, and the lion's mane and kingly status conjure mouth-watering maleness. Historically, the Peke hid out in the sleeves of pre-op trannies, known as eunuchs, and one of the breed's most famous stud dogs in England was named Ah Cum—a name only a gay man would dare say to Queen Victoria. Like gay men today, Pekes are superior creatures, filled with self-importance and exasperating stubbornness. Top breeder and handler David Fitzpatrick adds: "Pekes are for guys who always wanted to play with dolls . . . Pekes are for men who want an animal to fuss over and nurture. Aristocratic, entertaining, and fun loving are all qualities that would make a Peke endearing to anyone. However, you will seldom see a straight male who has a Peke unless it has been brought into the household by his wife. The Peke is a high-maintenance breed and requires 'someone to watch over him.' And you need the skills of a beautician."

Afghan Hound. It's not this dog's cloudy Middle Eastern origins that qualify him as a top gay dog. Hardly. It's his incarnation in the United States that reveals his rainbow of gay colors. Afghans are bigger than life: over the top, supernal, and superior. These aristocratic creatures are the Fabio of the dog world, the long-haired muscular top who makes every mere mortal subordinate to his desires. Afghans move with great style and a spring to their steps, like the fabulous queens who gallop in clogs behind them. Longtime fancier Allan Reznik shares his love of the breed: "Afghans are elegant from the tips of their Roman noses to the ends of their ring tails. With their exotic coat pattern, glamorous array of colors, aloof demeanor to the world, and floating gait, they make *you*, mere mortal, feel more graceful just being in their company. Guaranteed attention-getter and traffic stopper. A decorative grown-up's decorative pet. However, under all of that dripping silky coat beats the heart of an athlete, a hunter of leopard, and gazelle."

Pomeranian. Another ball of fabulous fur, the Pomeranian possesses qualities to which most gay men secretly aspire. He is a cocky runway model with an effervescent personality and a commanding presence; he is the life of the party and doesn't really like children. Spoiled Poms tend to be one-fag dogs and are aloof to straight neighbors, domestic staff, and other strangers. In the fatherland, the Pomeranian is sometimes referred to as the *Calvin Kleinerspitz.*

Lhasa Apso. In a word, divine! Yet, the question that stumps the Dalai Lama remains: How could Tibet, a land with nary a gay bar, come up with such an enchanting gay dog? The Apso's heavy coat, forming a veil over the eyes and feather duster of a tail, proves irresistible to gay men with fetishes for big hair and swishy tails. Owning an Apso is a near-religious experience for a worthy gay man: an Apso's trust and affection must be won; once bestowed, they are gifts that last many lifetimes.

THE GAY GROUP SYSTEM

Just as purebred dogs are categorized by the American Kennel Club, so too are purebred homosexuals categorized by ourselves, sociologists, book authors, and doormen at the Roxy.

These "types" are more flavors, colors, and styles that we choose for ourselves than stereotypes based on prejudice or divisive intentions. Each of these groups is a radiant band on our rainbow flag. The ever-encroaching dimensions of our PC world (and my genuine fear of the wrath of Sir Ian McKellan and Lady Bunny) compel this author to add that each of these gay types is coined in affection, admiration, and raunchy fun and desire. It is our wonderful differences, our many varied colors, shades, and hues that make our rainbow shine through storm after storm.

In reality, there are as many types of gay men as there are dog breeds under the heavens. How do gay men stereotype ourselves? Surely many guys out there fall into more than one of the categories and groups outlined in this book. For instance, lots of Opera Queens I know are self-proclaimed Size Queens—it's grand opera, with huge voices waddling on a Zeffirelli-size set! Show Tune Queens are often Homemakers, and one or two are Bears to boot. Likewise, we all know Twinks who have grown up to be Ladies of Leisure, Pump Boys, or even Homothugz. And, of course, most Fashionistas and Yentas are Chicken Hawks at heart.

It's time for a little gay soul-searching. Honesty and perspective, not specialties of the majority of gay men, will lead you to the most realistic assessment of your gay type. Unless you cut hair professionally; live on a ranch, beach, or runway; or wear six-inch heels on weekends; your type is likely less apparent. To assist you in your self-analysis, the author has devised a temperament test to help sort you out.

SIZE QUEEN
BEAR
LEATHERMAN
GAYSIAN
MAPLE LEAF FAG

TEMPERAMENT TESTS FOR GAY MEN

Temperament tests are commonly used by dog breeders to evaluate puppies for compatibility with their potential owners. Although simple, the tests reveal the personality and temperament of each puppy. They include exercises such as clapping to see if the puppy comes running, touching the puppy and basic petting, making loud noises, rolling the puppy on his back, and exposing the puppy to other animals.

The purpose of this section is not to temperament test puppies, but to temperament test *you!* If gay men were as simple as young, untrained puppies—and, yes, some yummy Biscuits are—life and love would be much easier. If you could just pet a gay man and roll him over on his back to see how he responds (!), you wouldn't need this chapter at all.

So, where do you fit in? How do you determine which type of homo best sums up your personality and temperament? Consider the following sections of questions to determine to which group you belong.

1 You belong to the **SPORTING GROUP** if you can answer yes to two or more of these questions:

___ Have you ever "pitch-poled"?
___ Have you ever had sex in a Jeep?
___ Is San Juan your favorite saint and city?
___ Are most of your shirts collarless or sleeveless?
___ Have you ever lost your shorts in an undertow?
___ Do you snap your head every time you hear the word *mariposa*?
___ Are you naturally blond, or do you prefer natural blonds?
___ Is tie-dye your favorite color?

SEE PAGE 47

2 You belong to the HOUND GROUP if you can answer yes to two or more of these questions:

___ Do you disdain plucking, shaving, and waxing?
___ Have you ever partied in a country that didn't speak English?
___ Have you ever been to a pride parade on a canal?
___ Did you grow up with a Beagle or a woman you called *Mamma*?
___ Do you visit the United States for long weekends?
___ Have you ever taken an "otter" to bed or hunted "wolf" off-season?
___ Does the term *bad puppy* make you think of dogs?
___ Have you ever been black and blue in October?

SEE PAGE 48

3 You belong to the WORKING GROUP if you can answer yes to two or more of these questions:

___ Do you go to the gym more than twice a week?
___ Do you kill time posing or lingering in the shower at the gym?
___ Can you run more than four blocks without getting winded?
___ Are you carb conscious?
___ Do you prefer white rice to pasta?
___ Do you spend more on dinners out than on your wardrobe?
___ Do you secretly consider yourself a "dogeater"?
___ Does your lunch include brioche, sushi, or a Powerbar?

SEE PAGE 49

4 You belong to the TERRIER GROUP if you can answer yes to two or more of these questions:

___ Does your favorite breed of dog have two legs instead of four?
___ Do you consider the age of consent a random law?
___ Do you feel liberals give fags a bad name?
___ Have you ever been to the Eagle or Bulldogs?
___ Are any of your exes *still* barely legal?
___ Do you think Condoleezza is a nice name for an adopted child?
___ Do you believe in the Juice Crew?
___ Do you belong to leatherdog.com?

SEE PAGE 50

5 You belong to the **TOY GROUP** if you can answer yes to two or more of these questions:

___ Do you repeatedly approach strangers in public places?
___ Do you require more attention than your three-year-old niece?
___ Do you actually *like* club music, and can you name more than one DJ?
___ Do you have saffron, herbes de Provence, or pie weights in your cupboard?
___ Have you ever ordered a nice brisket in Boca Raton or played the slots on Easter Sunday?
___ Are you carrying a credit card with another man's name on it (and does he know it)?
___ Do you club till 5 a.m. more than once a month?
___ Do you subscribe to more than one MSLO publication?

SEE PAGE 51

6 You belong to the **NON-SPORTING GROUP** if you can answer yes to two or more of these questions:

___ Have you paid more for one dress shirt than your sister pays for a dress?
___ Can you identify a Pucci from 100 yards?
___ Do you own more than twelve pairs of shoes?
___ Are you proud of your shoe size?
___ Can you name more than six Sondheim musicals in one breath?
___ Do you know the lyrics to "Sempre libera"? Can you sing it in Maria's key?
___ Can you put your mother's hair in a twist while reading *Vanity Fair*?
___ Can you swiftly convert nine inches to centimeters?

SEE PAGE 52

7 You belong to the **HERDING GROUP** if you can answer yes to two or more of these questions:

___ Do you have a preferred model for a lint brush?
___ Do you have a vacuum cleaner on every floor? Are they Dysons?
___ Have you ever spent an entire summer without air-conditioning?
___ Do you starch your sheets, iron your T-shirts, or pin your drapes?
___ Does a new John Deere get you in a plowing mood?
___ Do you wake up to the crowing of an actual cock?
___ Have you ever eaten a delish Cornflake for breakfast?
___ Have you ever been naked in a barn?

SEE PAGE 53

THE GAY GROUP LOOKING GLASS

Just as the AKC has its seven groups to categorize the purebred dogs the club recognizes, the QKC has its own group classifications for the men in our diverse community. You may see yourself, your lovers, your friends, and your colleagues through this rainbow-colored lens. Enjoy this voyeuristic tour of the world of queer men, but, Alice, be careful not to fall in!

Sporting Group Guys

OUTDOORSY, MANLY, NATURALLY COORDINATED, AND EAGER TO PLEASE

All-American Boy. Although your shirt is Ralph Lauren, your collar is always blue—or periwinkle. You are the easygoing guy-next-door type, whose smile would launch 1,000 Greek vessels. You are everyone's type, often the best friend, and lead a fairly stress-free existence.

SEE PAGE 58

California Boy. The golden boy of the Golden State, you are sporty, sensuous, and well oiled. A buff board, bod, and tan make you the Cali dream of queers the world over. Even sharks get their dorsal fins up for a fresh surfer blond like you.

SEE PAGE 64

Hombre. You are the dark Latin lover, the bonbon-shaking fan of the prince of Puerto Rico. You are as sensuous and impetuous as you are macho and bold. Your world is a spicy one, whether you're enjoying food, music, or men. You have flair in all you do.

SEE PAGE 86

Hound Group Guys

GREGARIOUS, VOCAL, SENSUOUS, AND LAID-BACK. TEND TO HUNT IN PACKS

Bear. Burly, furry, and masculine, you are the proverbial brown bear. You play rough and enjoy the hunt. Although outwardly gruff (as your tattoos advertise), most bears are of the teddy variety. You prefer the company of other hairy beasts—grizzly bears, polar bears, and on desperate nights, Gummy Bears.

SEE PAGE 62

Eurofag. Multilingual, bicontinental, and try-sexual, you live on *the* Continent, befriend metrosexuals, and trick with all-American acquaintances. You are sophisticated to an affected degree, articulate, and discerning in daylight. Eurofags wear Italian jeans and loafers, pilgrimage with DJs and orchestras, and despise the Kabbalah Madonna.

SEE PAGE 74

Maple Leaf Fag. You possess that "certain something," a *joie de vivre* from your French ancestors and sense and sensibility from your British ones. You are open minded, cheerful, polite, cultured, and unafraid to party in public. Canadians run the gamut of gay types, from petite pretty boys, Cowboys, and tattooed Bears to Hombres, Gaysians, and beyond. Blame Canada for gay marriages, gay adoption, and some of the gayest cities on the planet!

SEE PAGE 98

Southern Belle. Polite, pretty, and buxom, you are the toast of Tara! You shun the superficial and long for simpler times. Anything worth doing is worth doing properly and slowly, accompanied by cocktails, real friends, and good music.

SEE PAGE 106

Working Group Guys

INDUSTRIOUS, COMMITTED, STRONG, AND ENDURING

Gaysian. You are the next generation of power homos, the future Queens of Siam. Gay Asian men are among the most intelligent, resourceful, and professional fags in the universe. You can be headstrong, a little bitchy, and often too quick to judge. You have a sense of purpose, strong family values, and large expectations of friends and lovers.

SEE PAGE 80

Guppy. You are a grown-up City Girl with a job, living in and around your chosen metropolis. You are the Gay Urban Professional. You are efficient, a little trendy, and gainfully employed. You are one of the few, the proud, the Gentile lawyers, doctors, and bankers.

SEE PAGE 82

Pump Boy. Working out defines your being, and your being makes other gay men sweat. You are physical and committed. You thrive on structure and adhere to a commendable regimen of exercise, bodybuilding, and good nutrition. Clonish and maybe too perfect, your eight-pack abs and subtle chest glitter keep Chelsea and WeHo sweating and shining.

SEE PAGE 100

Terrier Group Guys

FEISTY, TOUGH, DETERMINED, BOLD, AND FEARLESS

Chicken Hawk. You crave youth and beauty, qualities you've lost or never had. You hunt, trap, and steal like a crazed fox. The white meat of your desiring is malleable, versatile, and a little bland—barely legal but always affordable. Remember that hawks can bite hard and sometimes eat their young. If you've got the pox bad, you better stay out of the coop.

SEE PAGE 66

City Girl. Young urbanette, you're sexy, snarky, and hardworking. Like the city itself, you never sleep . . . alone. You value social settings, whether dance clubs, neighborhood hangouts, or art exhibits. Anything that's fun and trendy gratifies this scenester clone. You have a real sense of community and act kindly toward the less fortunate, especially if they're hot, hung, or hammered.

SEE PAGE 68

Homothug. Buff, tough, and gangsta fab, you represent an elusive and enigmatic group. Your physical allure and bold masculinity fascinate and arouse; your ethnicity and inability to connect with gays or blacks makes you romantically untouchable to most gay men.

SEE PAGE 90

Leatherman. While you were born in swaddling cotton, you lean toward the hide of the beast. Dark colors, skillful accessories, and durable garments define you, a serious-minded, fun-seeking homo who enjoys being in complete control. Underneath the tough leather hide is a warm pink center: most leather queens are good hearted and genuine. Waste not, want not—you like beef and plenty of it.

SEE PAGE 94

Log Cabin Queer. Outspoken supporters of Bush, you are the reticent queer Republican. You're a member of the privileged class, and your sexuality has nothing to do with your political affiliation. You cherish your patriotism, your liberty, and your freedom. You'll proudly pay your partner's inheritance tax and remain gaily unmarried, if not actually single.

SEE PAGE 96

Toy Group Guys

POLITE, COURTEOUS, LADYLIKE, INDULGENT, AND DEMANDING

Homemaker. You are a stay-at-home fag, clutching a copy of *Martha Stewart Living* just to keep in touch. Your kitchen is a gourmet's wet dream, and your friends refer to you as the Barefoot Contessa. Happy to "put on the dog," you treasure your friends, your family, and the home that hosts them.

SEE PAGE 88

Lady of Leisure. You are the "chic" in chicken. You are a chicken living in an elegantly decorated roost, which you don't own. Your hawks are Wall Street roosters. You are content, carefree, and kept. You've never been more desirable or dangerous. You shameless sybarites have generous spirits, expensive taste, and good credit.

SEE PAGE 92

Twink. You are a club kid. A party doll. A boy toy. A tasty minx. You dance to the beat of your own DJ. You're living on Beijing time even though you reside in Chelsea and the Castro. The party starts at 8 a.m. You are social by definition, strive for attention, and need to feel popular and extremely desired. Twinks are survivors and always make the best of any bumps they encounter in the road.

SEE PAGE 108

Yenta. You're rich. You're talented. You're Broadway and Hollywood. You're the grown-up Jap: all hail the Jewish Queens and Barbra, your high priestess. You make classy if not kosher choices and run your life, and those of your disciples, with good sense and chutzpah.

SEE PAGE 112

Non-Sporting Group Guys

UNIQUE, RESOURCEFUL, CREATIVE, FRIVOLOUS, AND FLIPPANT

Drag Queen. High heels, big hair, and low camp, you are the royalty of the queer race. You are celebrities, performers, and soothsayers. You live to be onstage but may lose yourself when the footlights dim. Your bitchy exterior is as dense as your Wal-Mart mascara, and you know how to wear it out!

SEE PAGE 72

Fashionista. Look for the Gucci label. You are Fifth Avenue and Rodeo Drive. You have Donna Karan on speed dial and are nearly fluent in Italian (*Prada, Armani, ciao*). Label queens spend their lives on the runway, turning heads, tricks, and directions on a dime.

SEE PAGE 78

Hairdresser. You live for hair. It's not a profession, it's a ministry. Whether the medium is human hair or canine fur, you are an artist and craftsman. Twisting, teasing, and talking, you're tireless on your feet and miraculous with a bobby pin. Groomers are so artful and convincing, it's impossible to tell when you're "faking."

SEE PAGE 84

Show Tune and Opera Queens. You were born in Anatevya and grew up in Oklahoma; your parents were Floria Tosca and Mario Cavaradossi; your sisters are June and Rose. Life is big, colorful, and completely orchestrated. You cherish the Golden Age and claim to have attended Maria Callas's farewell performance as Lucia when you were "very, very young." You call all divas by their first names and connect every real-life situation with a show tune.

SEE PAGE 102

Size Queen. How do you measure a man's virtue? Very easily. You view the world keenly, sensitively . . . mathematically. You are a forward-thinking builder-upper. You seek skyscrapers and redwoods. Size Queens are unapologetically up front.

SEE PAGE 104

Herding Group Guys

RUGGED, RUSTIC, UNTIRING, AND WELL HEELED

Anal Perfectionist. Everything must be perfect from the bottom up. Tidy, immaculate, and obsessive about detail, you breathe easy only when your dust-free world is in perfect order: end tables leveled, sheets ironed, symmetrical creases in your 2wink boxers. Sometimes a *biotch*, you tend toward the control freakish and regularly rattle out commands at your friends and family.

SEE PAGE 60

Cowboy. You're one hard-riding rugged country dude who has captured the spirit of Americana and at least one well-spun Hollywood romance. You're hardworking, honest, and free spirited. Real-world cowboys may be too much man for the average ranchero to round up, saddle, and brand.

SEE PAGE 70

Farm Boy. You are robust and confident, exceptionally good natured, and skillful with a pitchfork. You're not afraid of real work and like to be active. You enjoy the outdoors, value home and family, and like to wrangle a good time. Your down-to-earth boyish qualities are exhilarating and enticing. Some Farm Boys are planters, and others are growers.

SEE PAGE 76

Two-Spirit. You are unique, wise, and fabulous with feathers. Gay Native Americans are the original gay Americans, although their parades never started with Dykes on Bikes. Named for their two-dimensional spirituality, gay Native Americans have been dubbed Two-Spirits, reflecting their masculine and feminine sides.

SEE PAGE 110

THE BAKERY ON AVENUE Q

Gay men are guilty of many sins, the least fun of which is ageism. We prejudge each other based on age, lie about our ages, and have hard-and-fast rules about what is the oldest man we'd ever date. There are three official categories of gay men*, based in part on their anticipated shelf life. The youngest and most edible are known as the Biscuits: these doughy twenty-somethings often rely on older gay men to look after them, to pay their way (and their rent), and to eagerly sip at their fountains of youth. Most Biscuits are trim and well groomed, although Southern Biscuits prefer more gravy than West Coast Biscuits. The next group of gay men is known as the Muffins, mid-thirty-somethings through forty-somethings. This group is enjoying the prime of their lives: making great money, enjoying life with a partner (and the occasional midnight Biscuit), and living in one or two homes that they own. The eldest group of gay men, the fifty-somethings, is known as the Scones. These high-cal retirees are the wisest and bitchiest of all homos, the silver daddies. Scones never admit to being over fifty-nine; no gay man has ever lived to sixty and disclosed it.

Here's the short list of dog breeds ideal for each group.

THE BISCUIT PUPS All of these breeds have youthful appeal and require lots of exercise and relatively little grooming to keep looking their best. Biscuits don't have a lot of expendable income, and keeping up the Biscuit lifestyle is exhausting and time consuming. They are ideal for boys on the go-go.

Australian Shepherd, Boxer, Cairn Terrier, Golden Retriever, Greyhound, Italian Greyhound, Japanese Chin, Pembroke Welsh Corgi, Pointer, Scottish Terrier, Toy Fox Terrier, West Highland White Terrier, and Whippet.

THE MUFFIN BREEDS These dogs require serious commitment to their coats, training, and upkeep, ideal for established gays in relationships or active guys who date, work, and play a lot. The Muffin breeds are fairly expensive to keep and require time and a stable home environment.

Afghan Hound, Bearded Collie, Bichon Frisé, Chinese Crested, Chow Chow, Cocker Spaniel, Irish Water Spaniel, Lhasa Apso, Longhaired Dachshunds, Miniature Poodle, Miniature Schnauzer, Old English Sheepdog, Shetland Sheepdog, Shiba Inu, Standard Poodle, Tibetan Terrier, and Wirehaired Dachshund; also any long-haired toy breed.

THE SCONE DOGS Here are the dogs who require less of their owners, who travel well (some of these are ideal snowbird dogs), and who appreciate the finer things in life. The Scone dogs are easygoing, not too demanding; some are expensive to acquire.

Affenpinscher, Beagle, Brussels Griffon, Bulldog, Clumber Spaniel, Dandie Dinmont Terrier, French Bulldog, Miniature Pinscher, Papillon, Skye Terrier, Smooth Miniature Dachshund, Toy Poodle, and Yorkshire Terrier.

**Footnote: Research based on exhaustive studies conducted by the Fred Mayo Boy Baker, LLC, New York, NY, May 2005.*

AVENUE Q BAKERY

MATCHMAKER: A–Z

How honest have you been in casting yourself in your gay-world type? Does anyone else think you're an Eurofag or a Pump Boy?

Just as wearing a leather cap on Fridays doesn't qualify you as a Leatherman, owning Queen Latifah's new album won't convince the boys on the Ave that you're a real Homothug. No gay man sees himself exactly as his friends and lovers see him. If your type isn't obvious to you, the simplest thing to do is to ask your best girlfriend (or any bossy bottom who knows you well) where you fit in. "Madge, am I a Bear?" You'll find out good and fast, Goldilocks, that you're a Guppy masquerading as a City Girl without a subway map. If you don't have a friend who can afford to be honest with you, you can consult a gay casting director—twenty minutes on the casting couch could be enlightening and refreshing. Some queens are too complicated for their own good; others are one dimensional or just truly dull. Perhaps you straddle a couple of categories—living on the cusp of Fashionista and Pump Boy, with definite Size Queen tendencies, sounds like an exciting, if exhausting, reality.

The author, applying his intimate knowledge of dogs and gay men, dutifully resumes the role of queer village matchmaker, what a Yenta would call a shadchan, to help you find your perfect canine match. Not every breed of purebred dog is right for every type of man, so let's take a careful look at our twenty-eight "breeds" of purebred homosexuals and consider which dogs best suit the lifestyle, personality, and temperament of each.

A quick note to readers who are still in the bookstore, likely standing in an aisle other than "Gay and Lesbian Studies": please don't cruise the illustrations. *Woof!* is a guide for men looking for the perfect dog (actual four-legged canine). This is not a find-a-queer-husband manual. As titillating as Mr. O'Malley's drawings may be, none of these men actually exists. Skimming the California Boy profile may indeed give you some helpful insight, but it won't net you a surfer for the weekend. You're free to peruse all twenty-eight profiles, even the ones you aspire to be/have/do, as long as you realize you can't really trap the Bear on page 63 or kidnap the Twink on page 109.

PASSPORT
BOY
TOY

ALL-AMERICAN BOY

The most popular breed in America is this Yankee Doodle's breed of choice, the Labrador Retriever. Recognizable and resourceful, Labradors speckle the countryside in yellow, chocolate, and black, swimming, running, playing, hunting, and excelling in every possible pursuit. Although incurably hetero, Labradors fit the All-American Boy's image of sporty, sensible, and handsome. An equally ideal choice is the Golden Retriever, the country's other popular retriever and sporting dog. Not as methodical and instantly trainable as Labs, Goldens are more sensitive and emotional. Goldens "think" before obeying, which is acceptable in a *four*-footed bedfellow. Both of these retrievers are devoted companions, although the Golden is sweeter and more glamorous with his longer, silky coat. A third retriever, this one made in America, deserves mention, the Chesapeake Bay Retriever. Far less common than the Lab or the Golden, the Chessie offers a marvelous alternative. The Chessie is more dog—larger, more courageous, and more protective, but equally loyal and responsive. Retrievers, like All-American Boys, live for oral stimulation: they need something in their mouths to be happy, be it a Frisbee, a bird, or just another bugle-boy buddy.

A few other sporting dogs fit the boy-next-door's bill of right dogs, including the Brittany, the English Springer Spaniel, and the German Shorthaired Pointer. For guys living in smaller homes, the Brittany and the Springer are excellent choices; both require much less space than a retriever. These are both biddable, bright companion dogs, with the Springer having more coat and elegance. The GSP remains a popular choice for a companion, as he's smart, is easy to care for, and loves a romp with a brawny pal. Who could resist? The Vizsla, the solid-rust pointing dog from Hungary, counts among the most versatile of sporting dogs, ideal for the guy on the go who likes outdoor activities. Vizslas also enjoy home life with their dads, proving to be among the most sensitive, loving, and devoted of all dogs. They are easy to care for, having short coats and few health concerns.

For the All-American Boy who likes a big, burly, and very hairy playmate, the Newfoundland makes a terrific choice. You couldn't find a sweeter fellow than this 150-pound barrel of muscle and devotion. A powerful swimmer and water rescuer, the Newf is the lifeguard of the dog world—how many gay boys can resist a bronze, furry fellow paddling toward them? Newfs come in brown, black, gray, and black and white.

For the All-American Boy who appreciates a tougher, harder companion, the Airedale Terrier can turn up the heat. Large for a terrier, the Airedale stands about as tall as a Labrador; he loves to work out and is very trainable. He's protective and loyal and doesn't admire strangers. In addition to hunting anything from geese to bears, this breed has experience in the armed forces. No healthy American boy could turn down a frisky cadet who's surprisingly big for his inches.

For the guy who's an experienced dog owner, the Dalmatian makes a colorful choice. Even though this Disney star is usually black and white, he's a clever, outgoing canine who needs an owner who's ready to keep up with his energy and enthusiasm for life—don't let his Non-Sporting classification fool you! For All-American Boys who are looking for a muscular, lithe, blue-eyed babe to share ski weekends and favorite winter sports, the Siberian Husky is just your spitz. Here's a gentle, easygoing fellow who will entertain and befriend you, although he's not going to protect you from a wayward bear (or a horny ski instructor who tries to break into your cabin—and that's OK, too).

ANAL PERFECTIONIST

Resourceful in every possible way, the Anal Perfectionist lives in a near-perfect world (often a high-rise condo or townhouse in the 'burbs), where the carpets are white, the linens and drapes match, and every pickle fork has its place. This is a queen with a mission: to survive she must be organized, fastidious, and industrious. To match her perfectly combed white carpet, the Anal Perfectionist has the perfectly coiffed Bichon Frisé, a nonshedding white dog who is bright and easily trained. The original bossy bottom, the AP queen needs to be in control; as such, she makes the ideal dog owner, as the majority of dogs like to find someone who will be master to her doggy slave. Like the Bichon, the Miniature Poodle is a scholarly home companion who hardly sheds a hair. Poodles offer many outlets for the AP queen to be creative and have the upper hand: few breeds are as patient and forgiving as the Poodle. If you want to dye the Poodles to match the kitchen curtains, they won't even mind; you can clip them to look like a pony, a lion, or a lawn sculpture—they're game if you've got the time and knack for clipping.

The Maltese and Shih Tzu make exceptional choices for the guy who likes pretty things in his home. Both breeds are ornate, sweet natured, and very trustworthy with your expensive accessories.

For the Anal Perfectionist looking for a breed with less hair, consider the fabulous Italian Greyhound, with his sleek coat and dainty ways, or the Basenji, adding a little African to your dwelling. Both are sensitive, smart dogs requiring an owner who is likewise. The IG is not the ideal dog for children, so you will have to safeguard your graceful little greyhound from your mauling nephew or your own child. Having escaped the Congo generations ago, Basenjis prefer homes without beasty little people. Neither of these dogs is a good watchdog either, but who cares? That's why God made doormen.

Larger breeds that fit the AP bill include the Portuguese Water Dog and the Samoyed. The Portie does not shed and is sporty and especially trainable. The Samoyed possesses a gorgeous solid white coat that sheds profusely, but most Anal Perfectionists have a DustBuster in every room and can easily keep up with this dog's down factory. The Sammy is prized for his good looks and winning smile, qualities that would make any AP flip with joy! A smaller version of the Samoyed can be found in the American Eskimo, long a popular companion in the United States from north to south. You don't have to live in Anchorage to be an Eskie 'mo!

BEAR

Unlike most gay groups, Bears wear their label as a badge of honor on their broad, hirsute chests. These hairy daddies are burly, furry, and fun—what everyone hopes a friendly bear will be! Although the ursine subculture includes a variety of shapes, sizes, and subsets, it's clear that Bears enjoy the company of other Bears, whether IM-ing, bowling, or playing Rrrough. Grizzly, polar, and brown, Bears are gregarious, easygoing, and cuddly.

For the Bear seeking an equally husky Bear, consider a bear-tracking canine such as the Cane Corso, the Akita, or the Karelian Bear Dog. All three are impressive and high intensity and probably more than enough dog for any Bear to handle. The Cane Corso, like the Bullmastiff and the even larger Neapolitan Mastiff, is a working breed that thrives as a protection dog. The Akita was indeed bred to hunt bear in Japan, although that is far from this beautiful, densely coated dog's twenty-first-century lot in life. The Karelian Bear Dog, for better or for worse, hasn't yet arrived in the present century and remains one of the most primitive domestic dogs known. Canadian Bears may be able to find such a dog, but it's not a dog for most people.

For papa Bears seeking to trap hairy boys—keeping trapping laws and any other laws in mind—the Otterhound is just that, a professional "otter" hunter. Young guys will love everything about this fun-loving dog, from the tip of his spongy nose to the twitch of his furry tail. A long-time favorite of Bears is the striking, tricolored Bernese Mountain Dog, the furry draft dog from Switzerland. As pups, Berners look like cubs themselves; as adults, they are steady, self-confident, and a bit aloof with strangers. When socialized, they are gregarious and fun-loving mates.

A favorite dog among Bears, historically used on badgers, if not otters, is the Dachshund. Because the Dachshund is clever, courageous, and sensible, Bears find this dog irresistible. Likewise, the Dachshund is tough on the outside and truly sweet on the inside (like most Bears themselves). Dachsies are also very intelligent and equally stubborn, like the majority of the Bears I've encountered in the woods.

For the Bear seeking a hot, hairy, and muscular trapper, an Irish Wolfhound or Borzoi is the hound for you, bred for centuries to pin a "wolf." These large-bodied hairy Greyhound-like dogs are sure to make a statement.

More to the heart of a Bear, the good-natured and affectionate Border Terrier is a picnic basket of a choice. As the breed standard puts it, "In the field he is hard as nails and game as they come." No Bear could resist those qualities. Another terrier who makes an ideal companion (to sit by your side while you're busy on your computer) is the Australian Terrier. This rough-and-tumble Aussie is naturally aggressive and confident in public and affectionate and good humored at home. He's described as a spirited "hedge hunter," so, ladies, mind your hedges! A true honey of a bear is the Chow Chow, which as a puppy looks like a bear cub indeed. Walk a Chow puppy through Boys Town and see if you go home alone! Chows need an affectionate master who will train them fairly and socialize them to become the good-natured, lovable teddy bears they should be.

For Bears on the prowl, a good scenting hound makes an ideal choice. The easygoing Basset Hound excels at sniffing out cubs, chubs, and cowbears, although they won't let you in the Dugout with him even if he's in a well-fitted harness.

bear

CALIFORNIA BOY

Who has more fun than this sinewy Peter Pan always questing for "the big one"? This West Coast sun god lives for the rays, the waves, and a long, exciting ride, and he wants a dog who thinks likewise. The sporting breeds offer many great choices for the California Boy. First on the list is the Portuguese Water Dog, with his waterproof coat and natural affinity for the surf. The Portie can take to the waves like a pro and enjoys spending hours on end at the beach. Any of the retriever breeds would also happily join in the fun, such as the easygoing Golden Retriever, the ready-for-anything Labrador Retriever, or even the light-hearted Flat-Coated Retriever. The Curly-Coated Retriever may be a little too serious, reserved, and intelligent for this gay blond to handle. Although the California sun might prove too strong for the Newfoundland, this burly, web-footed working dog can hardly be bettered in the water. He is the lifeguard of the dog world and makes the perfect mate for the über-surfer. And the Newf is one lifeguard who won't pretend he doesn't know you the next time you show up at Muscle Beach.

The Dalmatian certainly has the energy to keep up with the California Boy's lifestyle, as he's lively and virtually untiring, virtues every WeHo queen admires. Dals derive from sporting dogs and have drives similar to those of the retrievers.

Matching this gay boy's friendly, confident air, the Lakeland Terrier possesses a cock-of-the-walk attitude; he is lively and opinionated. Although the Lakey often bonds with one person, he forms his relationships on trust and mutual respect—an ideal choice for a California Boy who can't commit to a color, much less a breed or a cabana boy! Another option from the Terrier Group is the Norwich Terrier, whose adaptable, loyal temperament and gregarious nature would fit in well with a blue-state surfer colony. Lakeys and Norwich, like most of the terriers, are hardy and long lived, rarely needing veterinary attention. Cali Boys may attract some visitors from Down Under by adopting an Australian or Silky Terrier. Gay surfers are on the rise in Australia, and they'll be willing to teach you the finer points of "pitch-poling," "barreling," and "butt-breaching."

For the Cali Boy with a soft spot for Latinos, why not take home a Havanese? This miniature wonder comes in many colors and is very adaptable to the California sun, having developed on the sun-scorched shores of its native Cuba. For the surfie looking for a pup small enough to fit into his backpack while he's biking, either the Toy Fox Terrier or the Miniature Pinscher would make an easy-care, easygoing, easy-riding chum. Both of these breeds require hands-on training and discipline, or else they'll own you and yap all day until the whole coast knows it.

For a little something different, the dread-locked Puli simply has it all. This is a smart, vigorous, medium-size dog who's an affectionate and fun landlubber. The corded coat requires much less care than you might expect, and a Puli is a great conversation starter, especially when he's guarding your Jeep or beach towel.

CHICKEN HAWK

Chicken Hawks, like condors, turkey vultures, and other handsome birds of prey, are frequently maligned by society, although they are in fact just the victims of bad press agents (the bald eagle has a great one!). Chicken Hawks will never make the endangered species list, for they still can be sighted in large flocks around certain community colleges and trade schools. Occasionally, one Lone Hawk (of the Pink-tailed or Great Horned species) may be spied trespassing, but these avian outcasts hardly represent the whole community.

Chicken Hawks have a fun-loving, devil-may-care attitude toward the world around them and like dogs with a similarly youthful love of life. The Golden Retriever and the Nova Scotia Duck Toller are two fellow jubilant spirits, both outgoing, friendly, and good with children. No college jock can resist the wagging tail of the Golden Retriever. Another breed with great frat party appeal is the Bulldog, the perfect collegiate mascot. On weekends, a Bulldog is content to do nothing other than watch football with his boy band, eat corn chips, and fart without regret. Chicken Hawks are patient for their prey—in this case, curious college lads and other teenage broilers.

Equally irresistible is the Beagle, whose cute face, handy size, and happy temperament match the needs of most Chicken Hawks. Similarly, the Petit Basset Griffon Vendéen, or PBGV, ranks as one of the happiest of all dogs, as does the Cocker Spaniel, prized for his merry, outgoing ways.

From the Herding Group, the Bearded Collie, the Old English Sheepdog, and the Cardigan Welsh Corgi stand out as candidates. All of these breeds have a joyful quality to them that celebrates the fun side of life. We can't forget the Fox Terriers, both Smooth and Wire, both of whom would be content to dine on chicken nightly. The Fox Terriers are keen and lively, reveling in an owner who is easygoing, available, and entertaining.

Gay men who see themselves as Chicken Hawks may truly desire the long-term, unconditional affection of a well-chosen canine companion. The exciting pursuit of younger men often leads to disappointment for the easily gratified (readily dumped) Chicken Hawk. In truth, a faithful dog will serve as more than a capon magnet for the Chicken Hawk: he'll be that best girlfriend who will always be happy to lick your feathers back into place.

U
STATE

CITY GIRL

New York, Chicago, LA, Boston, Phoenix, or San Francisco: City Girls love dogs and usually make ideal dog parents. Doggy day care and dog walkers have made it possible for City Girls to live with many breeds of dog that wouldn't have been otherwise suitable. You might even say that in the big city, size doesn't matter (just don't say it too loud at Splash or the Eagle). The City Girl is better with an easygoing canine such as a Greyhound, a Great Dane, or a Boxer than with a dynamo such as a Border Collie, a Brittany, or a German Shorthaired Pointer. The least slobbery of the mastiff breeds, the Boxer looks good at the end of a leash and doesn't require too much room indoors. The Greyhound and the Great Dane, likewise, happily convert to futon spuds, lazing most afternoons in shifting sunspots.

For the City Girl seeking to attract rough military trade in the park, few breeds magnetize men better than the tall and handsome Airedale Terrier. If you're looking for a "don't-ask, don't-tell" bottom, select a sweet-natured smaller version such as the Welsh Terrier. (Giant Airedales have been known to scare femmy bottoms, even in the armed forces.) Keep both of these long-legged wirehaired terriers in their traditional *hard* coats for best results.

For a sweeter, close-bonding companion—because disco bunny knows how lonely the big city can be—consider the Cavalier King Charles Spaniel or the English Springer Spaniel. Both breeds excel in cities and are well-behaved apartment dogs. Coat care cannot be overlooked on either of these elegant spaniels, who have fringed ears, legs, and tails. The Shiba Inu has also become a top City Girl choice; this is a small dog with a big attitude. He is catlike in every respect except house-training. Shibas can be demanding and stubborn, firmly convinced they are your equal.

Small dogs naturally make excellent City Girl girlfriends. The Miniature Pinscher and Miniature Schnauzer, both sassy and spicy, continue to please the gayest of boys in Metropolis. There's a veritable school of them in Silver Lake alone! Both breeds are stylish, are portable, and travel nicely on the bus or subway. One of the most popular tykes in town is the Pug. This compact, easygoing pet dog requires minimal coat care and a temperature-controlled environment (aka, air-conditioning). WeHo and SoHo 'mos are well advised to avoid the designer-dog mutts that have been sideswiping straights for big dollars. Puggles, Yorkie-poos, and Pomapoos will soon go the way of the Furby but will cost much more before the fad is faded.

COWBOY

The great American West and those rugged cattlemen symbolize the sacred and untouchable in the red states. As gay Cowboys unashamedly confess, nothing on the ranch is untouchable. And, as far as the sacred goes, gay Americans are supplicating on bended knees, paying long overdue tribute to our free and brave bronco boys. "Don't fence me in" has become the new hymn of praise, and the rodeo is the hottest show in town.

For real-life gay Cowboys, few dogs will serve your needs better than a Border Collie or an Australian Shepherd, two talented herding dogs who can work both sheep and cattle. Country boys who work the ranch also favor hound dogs, and the quintessential working hound dog is the Louisiana state dog, the Catahoula Leopard Dog, able to work cattle and protect the flock from four-legged predators.

For rough-riding men looking to rope a smaller dog, the Jack Russell (or Parson Russell) Terrier makes an excellent riding partner, as they were bred small enough to fit into a saddlebag. The good Parson Russell didn't foresee our trying to squeeze them into purses or fanny bags! Regardless, he'd be glad to learn that gay Cowboys are very serious about riding.

For the Cowboy seeking a larger flock-guardian dog, consider the Anatolian Shepherd, the Great Pyrenees, or the Kuvasz, as any one of these will ably watch over your woolly charges while you're killing time with an inquisitive rancher or practicing your two-step with a skillful rodeo star. If you're butch enough to pull off hip boots, a leather jacket, and a motorcycle, you're probably man enough to handle the Bouvier des Flandres or the Australian Cattle Dog. Neither of these dogs will attract hot young cowpokes back to your tent, but you're bound to draw some competent lesbian farmhands to work the ranch.

The perfect Cowboy's dog may be a Corgi. There are two breeds of these Welsh dwarfs: the Pembroke Welsh Corgi and the Cardigan Welsh Corgi, the latter of which has a tail, rounded ears, and a less foxy expression. These are fun-loving, hardy farm dogs who will happily fit into a rugged outdoor life. The Corgis are expert cow dogs and instinctively know how to get out of the way of flying hooves. Now, that's a butch talent if there ever was one!

For the queer ranchero looking for a fishing buddy, the Spanish Water Dog is *perro numero uno!* This remarkable breed from Spain is the brightest, most playful, and easiest-to-train canine on the planet. He will work on the ranch, herd sheep, and then swim till dusk. This fishing buddy wants you to bring your *other* rod, the one with the line and reel on it. His claim to fame is that he's a scuba-doggy, actually diving under the water. The breed, known as Perro de Agua Español, is smaller than his cousin the Portuguese Water Dog and is fairly rare in the United States but worth the search.

An unlikely choice for a gay Cowboy is the designer dog known as the Puggle, a cross between a Beagle and a Pug; but if it's good enough to share a bed with Jake Gyllenhaal, we'll happily make an exception. Does anyone else wish he were a homeless Puggle looking for a straight actor's bed in Hollywood?

DRAG QUEEN

Royalty in the gay world, Drag Queens reign from dizzying heights . . . with their six-inch slingbacks and their hair teased close to God. Like wild dogs, Drag Queens are nocturnal in nature and howl with equal prowess—in nightclub acts they write, direct, produce, and star in themselves. Drag Queens rarely own dogs, unless their castles are staffed or their breakfast companions don't mind letting the dogs out before they leave.

Ironically Drag Queens are attracted to big-boned dogs with real hair—yes, the Standard Poodle and the Afghan Hound, for starters. Because Poodles in general are much easier to leash-train when you are wearing high heels, they are preferred to Afghans, who tend to tug. More so than almost any breed, Poodles can tolerate hours of brushing and fussing without complaint. White Poodles can even be dyed to match a Drag Queen's evening ensemble, and some Standards look very nice in mascara.

As elegant as the Afghan—though much less bitchy—is the Saluki, who has fabulous eyelashes and ear feathers and can model a whole array of earrings. Like Drag Queens in the big city, the Saluki subscribes to "survival of the fittest"; this is an adaptable, healthy running dog who doesn't require pampering or special care. Of course, the Saluki's graceful appearance and selective affection will win over the heart of even the evilest queen.

Looking for the perfect puppy to take to Wigstock or Fantasy Fest? You need a dog who can balance a *Hairspray* set piece on her head. A commonly overlooked gay breed is the Irish Water Spaniel, a curly-coated Poodle-like dog with a real sense of sporty fashion and a great sense of humor. The IWS practically wears a wig of his own locks on his head, and the breed's solid liver coloration makes him easy to accessorize. Don't forget daytime jewelry for those parade weekends!

For Drag Queens seeking dogs of royal backgrounds, like their own, or just smaller dogs to prop up their pillows, the Shih Tzu, the Maltese, and the Japanese Chin offer yards of silky tresses that require skilled and patient hair attendants. Any of these smaller breeds are a good fit for the Drag Queen who vows to get up by noon, as toy dogs handily can stow away in one's drag bag for an adventurous evening on the town.

For a little taste of Gay Paree, Drag Queens would be remiss not to consider the French Bulldog. Frenchies love to dress up, especially in feathery, girly apparel (even the boys!). They also enjoy a French manicure in a lively gay design. If you can dream up the outfit, the Frenchie can pull it off with ease. This is a fun-loving girlfriend who lives for glam.

For Drag Queens living on the wrong side of the tracks, none of the aforementioned froufrou diva dogs will do you much good when you're fighting for your purse on the avenue. Girlfriend, do yourself a favor and get a Rottweiler or a Doberman Pinscher. No one's going to mess with you when there's a fearless guard dog on the end of a thick leather lead, but be sure to wear flats or else you're going to snap a good heel.

EUROFAG

Eurofags are the postmodern gay Europeans, sophisticated, exclusive (except on weekends), and keenly stylish. The dogs that best fit these well-bred homosexuals derive from the Continent and travel well, fitting comfortably in an alligator carry-on for frequent transatlantic flights. Moneyed and lavish in their taste for the finest things, Eurofags live large and lush. They make de-lovely puppy daddies because they don't seem to work and they eat out in dog-friendly cafés. Of course, there are always those pseudo-Eurofags with Harrods's taste and Ikea pocketbooks, but it's all about appearances and looking the part.

For the Italian Eurofag, *il Piccolo Levriero Italiano* (Italian Greyhound) is slim, elegant, and portable, like the mobile phone ever attached to this queer's ear. The Bolognese, the silky-haired bichon from Bologna, makes a quaint choice, as he's sweet and personable. For the French Eurofag, the distinctive butterfly-eared Papillon (or his drop-eared brother, the Phalene; both varieties are also called Contintental Toy Spaniels) qualifies as the perfect first-class cabinmate. The French fags think they invented *le Caniche* (Poodle) the same night they came up with champagne, and there's no denying it. They remain loyal to Poodles to this day. *Le Bouledogue Français* (French Bulldog) may be too pop culture for the Eurofag today and would not summer very well in humid East Hampton.

The German and Austrian Eurofags prefer the smaller varieties of the Dachshund and *der Pudel* (Poodle) as well as the Miniature Pinscher and Affenpinscher, although the only good Affens come from America. The Belgian Eurofags, good looking but fairly rare, prefer their own Schipperke and *Griffon Bruxellois* (Brussels Griffon) breeds. From the original land of the dykes, Dutch Eurofags prowl around the canals of Amsterdam with pocket-size Yorkies, Poodles, and Brussels Griffons.

The Scandinavian Eurofags, who necessarily winter in the States since only sled dogs can survive that kind of cold, bring the Finnish Spitz, the Norwegian Elkhound, and the Swedish Vallhund. In fact, the Scandinavians produce such fabulous dogs that these fags have the best of many breeds, including the British terriers and the Poodles as well as many toy breeds.

The British Eurofags, better known as the Anglofags, prefer the easy and elegant (in men and dogs). Terriers such as the Norfolk, the Dandie Dinmont, and the Smooth Fox happily ride sidesaddle to these polo-shirted queens. A brilliant choice for the High Street Anglofags is the Yorkshire Terrier, a top toy on every continent. Many British pansies also adore the Asian sleeve dogs, including the Shih Tzu, the Japanese Chin, and the Pekingese. Tibetan Terriers, like their smaller Lhasa Apso cousin, are also favored. All of these dogs are colorful, are independent minded, and have no problem discerning a broad British accent.

The Swiss Eurofag, arguably the most highly bred of all Continental gays, can appreciate any of the handsome Italian, French, and German breeds we've already mentioned. Without a doubt, this Swiss missy demands the best of everything and shares his gourmet, designer, urbane palette with his pampered pooch.

PASSPORT

FARM BOY

A rare but wonderful breed is the gay Farm Boy—whether born into the nation's heartland or just a hired hand for hitching and hauling the harvest. This robust, hardworking guy is a man's man, and he requires an able canine to call his own. The hands-down choice for agricultural pursuits is the Border Collie, a breed known for its unstoppable work ethic and user-friendly trainability. Border Collies are moderate-size herding dogs who can adapt to any climate or task. The coat can be almost any length, with show pups boasting the longest, silkiest coats, and some farm dogs sporting shorter, flat coats.

Like the Border Collie is its American cousin, the Australian Shepherd, equally proficient and always attractive in his moderate-length, wavy coat, often colored in red or blue merle. This dog's blue eyes and sweet, loving ways can melt any Farm Boy's heart.

For a tougher and comparatively adaptable dog, the American Bulldog is a capital capitalist's choice, with its vigorous strength and eye-popping agility. This no-bull bully proves resourceful and trainable, a brawny protector and eager helper.

For the Farm Boy hoping to get lucky this season—with good weather, a bountiful harvest, and a few wild rolls in the hay—invest in the down and dirty Irish. Two able working dogs, the Soft Coated Wheaten Terrier and the Irish Terrier, promise companionship, a helping hand, and a warm body on nights when your luck is in a drought. Likewise, two smaller terriers, the Border Terrier and the Rat Terrier, are sensible choices that are happy to tag along on your tractor and will keep your silo vermin free. Neither breed is good looking, but who needs the competition on a lonely farm?

The herding dogs have long been favored for life on the farm. Besides the Border Collie and Aussie, the German Shepherd Dog and the Belgian Tervuren are ideal choices, provided you can find breeders who concentrate on working or trial lines. If you're looking for a pretty face to doll up the ranch, the Bearded Collie is happy to oblige. This dog is not going to run your livestock the way a Border Collie will, but he's bound to add a little bounce to your stride . . . and nothing gets Gay America's heart pumping like a little bounce on a well-built Farm Boy.

FASHIONISTA

These girls are on the cutting edge of fashion, style, and the *nouveaux*. They seek what is the trendiest, most fabulous, splashiest at the moment. Inevitably, the list of which breeds will suit their whims will vary with the dog in vogue or in *Details*. It may depend upon which breed the most popular chanteuse or Hollywood diva is stuffing into her Gucci bag or walking on the end of her rhinestone leash this week.

Like Cartier, Ferrari, and Barbra Streisand, the Bichon Frisé never goes out of style, ever since it made its way into American show rings in the early 1970s. Nonetheless, other spinoffs, although all long established, are starting to catch on. For example, the Coton de Tuléar is a perfect choice for today, as the breed is just finally being pronounced in the United States after rolling off the tongues and beds of Parisians for many years. By origin, the Coton hails from Madagascar. Other bichons worth mentioning are the Bolognese, an Italian breed named for Bologna but no doubt seen in Milan, too (and once the powdered pooch of Miss Marilyn Monroe), and the Havanese, a Cuban as cute as any South Beach bartender. Another favorite mascot of style mavens is the Maltese, whose silky white coat drapes to the floor and whose dark button eyes can melt even the bitchiest of Fashionistas. Case in point, the ever-so-perceptive Cojo carries one around as his muff.

Fashionistas cherish what is rare and hard to find, so any hot rare breed will suit their longings. Some top-shelf recommendations are the Alaskan Klee Kai (a small Husky-like beauty), the Azawakh (the most elegant greyhound you've ever seen, originating in Mali), the Braque du Bourbonnais (a stylish French pointer for the active queen), the Cesky Terrier (a short-legged terrier with a silky coat and a perfect temperament for the true Bohemian Bohemian), the Entelbucher (a miniature Swissy), the Japanese Spitz (a lovely variation on the American Eskimo Dog), the Pumi (a feisty little dog with great ears), the Spanish Water Dog (a sensational, smart, perfect, Poodle-like dog!), and the Tibetan Mastiff (a large long-coated working dog of great dignity).

Fashionistas can also consider some lesser known (if not rare) breeds that remain the best-kept secrets in the fancy, including the Papillon, the Dandie Dinmont Terrier, the Japanese Chin, the Tibetan Terrier, and the Tibetan Spaniel.

Fearless Fashionistas can also pick the breeds that will never go out of style: these include the Pekingese, the Afghan Hound, the English Setter, the Whippet, and the Toy Poodle. The current trend for designer dogs may seize the attention of less keen style-crazy homos, although it's not likely Puggles or Malti-poos will last the test of time as your Louis Vuitton or Bichon Frisé has.

GAYSIAN

The fabulous tribe of Gaysians is loved by non-Asians who call themselves Rice Queens, Curry Queens, and Glass Noodle Queens, each affectionately named for the kinds of men they prefer.* The politics of the queer Asian world make for sticky relations, although many Gaysians are devoted dog lovers, and many wonderful purebred dogs make exceptional choices. The East has produced (and exported to the West) some of the most fascinating dogs, and many gay Asians adore the breeds that link them to their homelands. Among these are the Thai Ridgeback, the Chinese Shar-Pei, the Korean Jindo, and the Japanese Tosa and Akita—all strong-minded, powerful dogs who tear asunder the manservant Ping image. Asian queens with these dogs are power queens, looking to stake their claims for their imposing virility.

Artists in Japan and China spent centuries creating tiny wonders—in porcelain, precious stones, and plant life—not to mention beautiful, perfect miniature dogs. The Japanese Chin is an exceptional little dog, ideal for the Gaysian who likes large sleeves and elegant ornamental dogs. Other superb examples of Asian miniature wonders are the Shih Tzu, the Pekingese, and the Pug.

The Shiba Inu, like the Akita, derives from Japan and is the most popular native breed in that country. Shibas have the attitude and presence of a Shinto god. They are likewise fearless and beautiful. Of all the Japanese breeds, the Shiba brings its unmistakable Eastern mysticism to Western shores and has remained unchanged for centuries. They are smart, clean, and efficient, like Nippon itself.

Some Potato Queens fancy breeds that derive from the West, including the Boxer and the German Shepherd Dog. Both of these breeds are highly regarded in the East, and many prominent American breeders have exported top dogs. The Boxer's elegant and unmistakable masculine air holds appeal for many proud Gaysians. The Boxer male bonds deeply with his owner, with an affection that is ineffable and gripping. The German Shepherd's temperament reflects an Asian sensibility: he is direct and fearless, confident and somewhat aloof, not lending himself to immediate or indiscriminate friendships.

For Gaysians who delight in the tiny, three fabulous toy dogs who enjoy long-standing fancies in the East meet the criteria: the Toy Poodle, the Pomeranian, and the Yorkshire Terrier. These toys are intelligent, sensitive, and discerning animals who have countless admirers in the East. Gaysians make ideal owners for these toy dogs, who love to be pampered, primped, and puppied.

**Footnote: These "types" are largely defined based on the starches consumed in the land of origin. Gaysians who date white guys are called Potato Queens, those who prefer Italian men are commonly called Pasta Queens, and those who chase guys from northern Italy are known as Polenta Queens. Gaysians who date Hispanic boys are known as Yucca Queens. Other variations include Orzo Queens, Couscous Queens, and Egg Noodle Queens.*

GUPPY

Out in the outskirts, Guppies swim to their city jobs daily—usually by train, ferry, or luxury car. Yes, Gay Urban Professionals—the fags with Jags—lead perfect queer-as-folk lives. Affluent and effortlessly cosmopolitan, Guppies make perfect puppy parents, as their sizable expendable incomes can pamper even the most demanding canine baby. Grooming salons, doggy day care, dog walkers, and obedience schools are in the future of any pampered pooch fortunate enough to call a Guppy "Dad."

Given gay men's fascination with tiny Asian dependents, the Shih Tzu wiggles to the top of the heap. This rapturous Chinese doll may be the most affectionate and loving of all breeds. The Japanese Chin, whose origins are actually Chinese, too, is the runner-up in this category. Both of these Asian adoptees are considerably more affordable than the two-legged variety, easier to acquire, and cheaper to educate. Not to mention that your Shih Tzu won't have to explain her two daddies in her first oral report.

Because Guppies inexorably tend toward the trendy, the dog of the moment always captures their fancies. Among the most popular small-dog choices are the Cavalier King Charles Spaniel, the Pug, the Pomeranian, and the Miniature Pinscher. This quartet of accessory pups are adaptable, fashionable, and portable—the iPods of the canine world. The Guppy looking for a less predictable small dog should take a peek at the English Toy Spaniel (called the Charlie by his friends), the Brussels Griffon, and the Affenpinscher.

A perennial favorite for the gay urbanite is the Golden Retriever, a true family dog whose personality is 100 percent rainbow—all inclusive, all love. Another family dog is the Bernese Mountain Dog, who's more protective than the Golden Retriever and not as overtly friendly to strangers. This beautiful tricolored dog is one of Switzerland's mountain-dog breeds, and he bonds very closely with his master and his master's inner circle. Like the Golden, he's earnest and sincere, qualities every gay man pretends to cherish.

Guppies also value efficiency, something that the terrier clan epitomizes. The Norfolk Terrier, the Smooth Fox Terrier, and the West Highland White Terrier are popular choices for city dwellers. A less common terrier, who matches his muddy-pawed cousins in personality and panache, is the Dandie Dinmont Terrier. Don't let his silken topknot and iconic dignified air mislead you: he's a bold, tenacious little dog with undeterred sporting instincts.

HAIRDRESSER

Hairdressers, whether professional or devotional, love the excitement and fulfillment of creating beauty through hair, be it human or canine. The world of dogs presents many rich opportunities for hairdressers (and groomers) to express their art. Many of the prospects have awe-inspiring coats; leading the list of such canines is the Afghan Hound. Here is a gay dog if there ever was one. In fact, the American Kennel Club standard describes the breed's temperament as, "Aloof (*bitchy!*) and dignified (*stuck-up!*), yet gay (*!*)." What queen could resist the Joan Crawford of canines (except that the Afghan is pretty and not even boy Afghans are as butch as Joan)? The breed is adorned with long silky hair, which is actually not clipped or trimmed, but you can bet you need a professional blow dryer for this aristocratic beauty. Of course, there are smaller dogs that can fulfill the Hairdresser's desires as well: the Lhasa Apso has floor-length hair, even longer than early Cher, and requires the full treatment, including curlers, bobby pins, barrettes, and gallons of conditioner. The Lhasa's Oriental cousin, the Shih Tzu, is a bit smaller but equally demanding in his hairstyling requirements. Both of these delectable darlings come in a rainbow of colors and are counted among the most affectionate of dogs. The all-white angel known as the Maltese can satisfy the Hairdresser's desires, too, as he's as well mannered as he is high maintenance.

Let's move on to the dog with the most abundant coat in the world, the international symbol of the flawless show dog, and one of the gayest of all breeds: the Standard Poodle. Make no mistake, the Standard Poodle is a sensible, intelligent, and athletic dog, but his coat requires an Olympic squad of stylists and poufers. Another contender for the Hairdresser's dog is the Cocker Spaniel, known for his merry (*gay!*) temperament and his ever-growing, ever-flowing coat in a rainbow of colors.

To mix things up a bit, Hairdressers may like to take on the Puli, covered head to toe in cords (not unlike Whoopi's dreadlocks). By nature—and who can blame him—the Puli is a bit suspicious of strangers, makes a good watchdog, and loves to be at home with his family.

On the other side of the canine hair chart are the terriers. Many of these breeds require great skill and panache to keep up: consider the Bedlington Terrier, in his lamblike garb; the Wire Fox Terrier, in his crisp, hard coat that never slights perfection; and the Kerry Blue Terrier, in his unique coloration and 'do.

Two other exceptional companion dogs with coats bigger than those of the Gabor sisters are the Bichon Frisé and the (rough) Chow Chow. Both breeds have had loyal gay followings for years, and the Bichon, like the Maltese and Poodles, may be the best answer for the Hairdresser with allergies, as the coats are single and do not shed. The Chow Chow is prized for his aloofness, although in reality he should be a friendly, well-socialized dog who enjoys his role as companion, watchdog, and eye candy.

Lastly, for professional Hairdressers, who spend ten hours on their feet each day in a salon, the best possible choices for you are none of the dogs we've mentioned! Who the hell wants to do hair at home after dealing with the rats' nests of clients all day? The Whippet—elegant, easy to care for, and no locks to speak of—or the smaller Italian Greyhound or the Miniature Pinscher have lots of attitude and require nothing more than a chamois!

HOMBRE

Latinos, Chicanos, Muchachos, Mexicanos, Cubanos, and Chalupas! Hombres are as varied as gay men themselves, although our idealized Latino and Chicano man is a hypermasculine, sensuous creature who embraces both his gayness and his ethnicity. The ideal dog for the Papi Chulo depends upon his personality and outward persona. Two truly gay breeds derive from Latin America: the Chihuahua and the Havanese. The Chihuahua, the petite dog wonder from Mexico, is more than a dog—he's a fashion accessory. Weighing in from one to six pounds, this pocket pup emits Chalupa pixie dust from his every pore. The Havanese comes from Cuba and is named for the nation's capital. A colorful bichon-type dog with a nonshedding coat and a lustrous personality, this Cuban doll is a great favorite with gay and straight owners across the United States. Check out the boys in South Beach (SoBe) or Little Havana. A third Hispanic breed possesses great machismo appeal, and its historic use would make any gay man sit up and say, *"¡Ay Dios mío!"* Developed to track down runaway prisoners (hot bad-boy Latinos!), the Dogo Argentino is a powerful, solid-white hunter whose man-trailing abilities rival a pack of Drag Queens at Cinco de Mayo.

A more attractive but equally macho dog is the Boxer. Here is the Latin connoisseur's dog: at once elegant, powerful, and rippling with energy, a real lover of a purebred dog. For the Papi looking for *el perro de perros,* that dog is, no doubt, the American Staffordshire Terrier. The most courageous dog on the planet (as his scrappy American Pit Bull Terrier cousins will attest, in English and in Spanish), the AmStaff is well put-together, stocky, and powerful for his inches. Talk about *cojones!* What Hombre or cha-cha queen can resist nineteen inches of solid beef?

Speaking of compact and well put together, the Dachshund continues to be a favorite in the Latino community; few dogs can compete with the resolve and single-mindedness of the Dachshund. Like the AmStaff, the Dachshund requires a firm but fair hand for training.

As Latinos are fond of water sports, beaches, and cabana life, the Golden Retriever proves a crowd-pleasing favorite, and how lucky is the Golden living "La Vida Loca," sharing a bed with Puerto Rican god Ricky Martin?

For the fearless papacito, who's not projecting his machismo on his pup, let's look at some appealing dogs with flair and style. The Whippet cannot be outraced for grace and elegance. In essence, the Whippet is the miniaturized, perfected form of the Greyhound. Like an ideal Latin playmate, the Whippet is sensitive and gentle but capable of great intensity in the heat of the moment. For flair and hair, we have the Yorkshire Terrier, the Lhasa Apso, the Cocker Spaniel, and the Poodle. This quartet of coated goddesses can raise the creative Hombre to new levels of divinity.

HOMEMAKER

The recipe for this happily homebound homo is one part Donna Reed, one part Martha Stewart, and two parts well-to-do life partner. There's truly nothing like a wealthy husband to make this gay man squeal, "There's no place like home!" Homemakers make the most of their gay domiciles, excelling at cooking, gardening, entertaining, shopping, decorating, and accumulating American Express bonus points.

The family dog is selected with a theme and a color scheme in mind. A matching pair of the perfect breed is even better, as it adds symmetry and distinction to the home. A matched pair of French Bulldogs, for instance, can hardly be bettered. Like collecting prewar Wedgwood or Fiesta dishes, having a pair of Frenchies is living kitsch. Alternatively, as an homage to the Divine Domestic Diva's original breed, a pair of Chow Chows (Rough or Smooth) expands on an Asian theme and looks beautiful indoors on your imported Indian wool and silk tapestry or outdoors in your expertly pruned Zen garden. Another Asian favorite is the Shiba Inu, the smallest of Japan's spitz breeds, a popular choice for high-rise city dwellers. The Shiba is an elegant, fun-loving dog who adds depth and life to any loving household.

The English Toy Spaniel, affectionately called the Charlie, makes a lovely addition to a British-inspired home decor. Charlies have puggy faces and gay temperaments. Consider getting four of them—one in each of the accepted color patterns—to complete your gay royal family. Most Homemakers are devout collectors, so locating breeders of all four colors will be a rewarding challenge.

Chihuahuas, perfect for a southwestern theme, are fun to collect, too, and their color variations are endless. Homemakers also profess an affinity for Dachshunds, for a touch of the Continental. Miniature Dachshunds, in particular, excel in braces (pairs) and make devoted, intelligent companions. Keep them away from your flowerbeds, as they can botch up your landscaping worse than a drunk lesbian with a backhoe.

Two other lovely choices are the Bichon Frisé and the Tibetan Spaniel. In addition to his heavenly appearance, the all-white Bichon Frisé does not shed, which is a plus for the Homemaker who'd rather shop than run the Electrolux. The Tibbie, closely related to the Peke, is a neat little dog whose charm and beauty complement any well-kept home.

Happy Birthday

HOMOTHUG

Homothugz are tough, masculine guys who work hard to project their desired look. *Homothug* is about strength, attitude, and size—it is way more than just a "black thing." (Truth be told, most gay black men don't fit into this elusive category, and some white Brooklyn boys and LA Latinos do.) The image of this Cocoa Puff Daddy pulses with originality: the music is hip-hop; the jewelry, like the man himself, is flashy and solid; the clothes are loose; and the body is tight.

The obvious first-choice canine for this urban demigod is any well-made breed of bully dog, the dogs of bull and terrier type. The American Pit Bull Terrier, known as the American Staffordshire Terrier on Madison Avenue, like the Thugz themselves, gets a bad rap, especially from that uptown club (aka AKC). Real Pit Bull lovers call their dogs bulldogs, and when you're in Atlanta you'll find a lot of hot *brothas* at Bulldogs. Pit Bulls can be the most reliable, versatile, and trainable dogs on the planet, but when mistreated, poorly bred, and carelessly trained, they can be the most dangerous and unpredictable "bad dogs" on the block. A sharp Pit Bull with its rippling musculature and no-nonsense looks cuts the perfect image for the Homothug.

The Staffordshire Bull Terrier, equally sharp and trainable, can't compete with the Pit Bull's athleticism and determination, but taking second place to a Pit Bull's no small feat (if you live to tell about it). The American Bulldog, unlike the more common English breed, can stand taller than any of the bull and terrier types and is equally impressive in physique, agility, and strength. This Bulldog is hardcore through and through, a prime homeboy candidate. Among the working dogs best suited and liked are the Neapolitan Mastiff, the Rottweiler, the Akita, and the Doberman Pinscher. As unlikely a choice as a Mafia boss, the Neo frightens even straight boys. None uglier, none scarier. Covered in wrinkles and slobber with calluses on his knees, the Neo is the troll of the dog world. Black and tan in color and smooth coated, both the Rottie and the Dobie project that fearless but good-natured air. These two thick Germans exude strength, size, and style. The Akita, the largest of Japan's spitz dogs, has an intensity and swagger that will impress any Chocolate Daddy who doesn't mind giving his dog a shape up. Unlike any of the smooth-coated choices we've mentioned, the Akita has a long double coat that sheds profusely. Of all of these breeds, the Akita is the most independent minded and is not a choice for amateur dog people.

The Giant Schnauzer cuts an impressive image with his sleek black coat, rock-hard body, sloping neck line, and cropped ears. One look at this dog's bearded face and flashy silhouette, and you know that this dog belongs to a fly Homothug. Belgian Malinois compare favorably with German Shepherd Dogs, still known in certain circles as police dogs. The Malinois is less common but equally successful in competitive trials, military and police work, and other "guy guy" pursuits. If your rims and chains aren't getting you noticed by that bangin' cop on the down-low, surely this enviable K-9 will help your case.

LADY OF LEISURE

This lucky tribe of former Pixies, tramps, and Twinks are lounging in temporary luxury. The "near Mrs." of established gay husbands, the Ladies of Leisure have time (and rented jewelry) on their hands—and little time for anything except the gym, lunch, cocktails, shopping, and signing for packages. For the Lady of Leisure who is a dog lover, only a fabulous showy dog cuts the Grey Poupon. Select a breed that sits well for portrait artists and sculptors. The Italian Greyhound can outpose any dog, with her elegant lines and well-chiseled head. The Papillon also excels in the ornamental. Surely any petite breed that drips such ferocious swellegance makes an ideal subject. The Maltese, the Shih Tzu, and the Lhasa Apso can rival even the most indulgent Ladies Who Lunch when it comes to lounging, looking exquisite, and lapping up heated cream from Limoges saucers.

For most of the duchesses in this category, size matters more than substance, but extra large requires more effort. There's nothing leisurely about caring for a Great Dane or an Irish Wolfhound, and who wants to squeeze a pony into a private elevator? Think teeny for a change, and adopt a minuscule Miniature Pinscher, Yorkshire Terrier, or Chihuahua (preferably a Longhair in an unusual color or pattern). Any one of these mites will happily accompany you around town and will look more than fabulous in that Hermès bag that took nine months to come in.

For more exotic and expensive tastes, consider the Dandie Dinmont Terrier and the Skye Terrier. When well bred and well groomed, evasive qualities that every Countess of the Couch strives for, these two darlings add a level of sophistication to an otherwise dim Leisure diva and help to perpetuate the illusion of old money. Most Ladies of Leisure have neither old money nor new money—they have other people's money. (And in special circumstances they have lottery money, the worst kind of money of all!) The Tibetan Terrier, a grander, more expensive version of the Lhasa Apso, will happily laze and glaze with the Lady of Leisure. Like all of the veiled wonders on this roster, the TT requires extensive grooming. Be sure to schedule weekly appointments at a salon near your own day spa or arrange for a car service. With your freshly styled Tibetan or Apso, you'll be the toast of WeHo.

The sighthounds, when given adequate exercise, make exquisite additions to the Lady of Leisure's dwelling. The Whippet, the Borzoi, and the Scottish Deerhound lend an air of Old World sophistication and Victorian swank to any Upper West Side dive. Two perennial darlings of the day, the French Bulldog and his English uncle, the Bulldog, prove to be utterly domestic and fun to spoil. Like the Lady of Leisure herself, both of these Bulldogs enjoy expensive bonbons and slumming downtown for an occasional matinee.

LEATHERMAN

Once an underground fashion statement, leather has come a long way since the days of secret campouts during which queer bikers and G.I. Josephines hooked up. Today Leathermen are a part of a thriving gay community that embraces a sensibility that transcends a mere uniform. Leather is proudly worn by queers of many different cultures, classes, and lifestyles. Leathermen exalt in the differences yet always identify themselves by the attire they earn: boots, jackets, chaps, vests, caps . . . and sometimes collars. (Woof!)

As varied as the community is, so too is the gang of canines that appeal to Leathermen. There's no doubt that the two top choices are sporty, fun, and sexy: the Bull Terrier and the Staffordshire Bull Terrier look good in leather! These two rugged dogs, both of whom descend from fighting-dog ancestry, are tough and sensible. For the alpha Leatherman looking to make an impression, few dogs can compare with the Giant Schnauzer, a rugged, hardy, working guard dog who looks best when he's in solid black. Another option is the Bouvier des Flandres, a distinctive cow dog from Belgium. Leathermen have an affinity for all things cow, and this Bouvier can bring home the filet. Like fur queens and other carnivores, Leathermen despise PETA and all that it represents. This virulent group opposes using animals for meat and clothing as well as having pets. Keep your paws off my Bouvier and my Jackie mink hat, too!

Because leather is also about spirit and playfulness, the Dachshund embodies the Leatherman's credo: a low-to-the ground German who's happy to be your dogboy. Known for their perseverance and courage, Dachshunds prove to be fun-loving canines with lots of heart and soul. Some Dachsies even have a fetish for boots, both licking and chewing. The breed lives to dig, and rolling in mud comes naturally. Another terrific Leatherman choice is the dog known as *multum in parvo* (a lot in a little): the Pug offers a lot in a small package. The Pug's body is compact and muscular, and as a companion he's dignified, outgoing, and even tempered.

If a Nordic dog appeals to the Leatherman, then the Siberian Husky can lead the pack. Here is a sensitive and friendly canine who is hardworking and looks great in a harness! Huskies thrive in colder climes with active owners who like to get out and enjoy life. They're too big to ride on a motorcycle, but they'll happily run next to your bike.

For Leathermen who prefer a smaller dog, two toy dogs make excellent candidates: the Miniature Pinscher and the Affenpinscher. Both breeds have irrepressible spirits and love being the center of attention. Unlike some toy breeds, the MinPin and the Affen enjoy masculine camaraderie and doing big-dog things, even though the Affen has a beguiling sense of camp, à la Bette Davis.

For the leather queen looking for a canine pal to share his leather journey, a Bulldog continues to be one of the most traditional choices: he is the authentic devil dog, *der Teufelshund,* the symbol of the ever-faithful, ever-hard marine corps. Not only does the Bulldog look good in a leather cap, but he's also a sweet, genuine soul who's become that way from generations of hard living and underground activity. And just like his leather-clad master, he's a little misunderstood.

LOG CABIN QUEER

This just in: GOP is now the Gay Old Party. What's more farfetched than gay cowboys and queer Indians? Homosexual Republicans, of course! Not as numerous as flashy berdache Native Americans, Log Cabin Queers are painting our rainbow red, and bully for them! Let's begin our canine selection first by looking south. How about a coonhound from one of our good old Bible Belt states? The Black and Tan Coonhound is the quintessential hunting dog; he's got class, beauty, and lots of rugged appeal. If your log cabin has a live-in closet, then this coonhound is sure to fool your neighbors. If your log cabin is in the Lone Star State, or if you're still siding with "W," how about adopting a Blue Lacy, the state dog of Texas! This is an active herding dog indigenous to the American South that defines loyalty, single-mindedness, and other good Republican values.

Log Cabin homos are looking for dogs who capture the spirit of family values, thus any home-loving family dog will make an exceptional choice. The English Springer Spaniel was the choice of the senior Bush clan, and Millie served well as the nation's First Dog. The Golden Retriever and the Pointer are bright and lovable companions who are easily trained gundogs (ideal for the next time you take your attorney quail hunting). Other popular family dogs are the West Highland White Terrier and the Collie. More devoted, spirited family dogs can hardly be found.

Some good all-American breeds might serve equally well, such as the Chesapeake Bay Retriever, although Maryland rarely votes red, and the Boston Terrier, from the even bluer state of Massachusetts. If you can find a nice oversize Boston Terrier with a sour expression and an unyielding annoying bark, you can name him "Ted" and take photos of him hiding his bone.

GOP queers attracted to smaller, more dramatic dogs should consider the Brussels Griffon and the Affenpinscher. These miniature terrier-like dogs are comical and highly entertaining, behaving much like the monkeys they resemble. And you can name yours "Bonzo."

Once the symbol of the Democratic Party's unbeatable candidate, the Scottish Terrier has gone from the faithful "Fala" at FDR's side to the symbol of the junior Bush regime. Like "W," the Scottie has resolve and determination, along with a piercing, particularly "varminty" expression, living up to his nickname "the Diehard."

MAPLE LEAF FAG

Out and proud, gay Canadians parade wildly with their rainbow flags snapping in the breeze. Admittedly, the native Canadian dog breeds as a lot are too butch for the average gay man. The boys to our north look to their British, French, and American counterparts for their canine inspirations. Even so, we'd be remiss not to mention the maple leaf dogs by name.

Canada's own sporting breed, the Nova Scotia Duck Tolling Retriever, looks like a miniature Golden Retriever with lots of personality and ability. This duck buddy is no fair-weather friend: he likes to go out in rain or shine. Any outdoorsy, active Canadian boy looking for a versatile companion will instantly fall in love with this tail-swishing blonde. Another favorite Canadian breed is the Newfoundland, a strong, powerful, long-haired swimmer type, sure to delight a sporty 'mo. The Labrador Retriever, one of the world's most popular breeds, hails from Canada but may have too much piss and gusto for the cosmo-swilling cosmopolitan boys from Toronto and Montreal. The Canadian Eskimo Dog is a hairy, raunchy, primitive beast—*très sauvage*—too much dog for even a rugged Canadian Bear to handle, aye.

The boys in Toronto embrace the steel and blue wonder known as the Yorkshire Terrier, a toast to their British forebears. In Vancouver, the city boys are sleeping with Shih Tzu and Chihuahuas and other hairy beasts. As in American cities on both coasts—New York and Boston in the East and Seattle and Portland in the West—these smaller breeds are all the rage, and the Maple Leaf Fags are toting them around in French leather and British suede.

Other more active Canadian boys, the gym bunnies and other buff-tailed hotties, are keen on the popular sporting breeds, including the Brittany, more of an American dog than a French one, as well as two Euro faves, the Weimaraner and the Vizsla. And surely that Halifax Toller would make an excellent alternative to the ubiquitous Golden Retriever, but this perennially sunny gundog continues to rank high on the charts.

Retired Greyhounds have many gay advocates in Canada, and a number of couples find these intelligent, easygoing hounds ideal companions. The gay Cowboy and Bear aren't exclusive to American soil; the Canadians have their tribes and packs of these guys. The Australian Shepherd, the Shetland Sheepdog, the Rottweiler, and the West Highland White Terrier make fun knockabout chums for many rugged Canadian men.

PUMP BOY

Committed to their own physical perfection and health, Pump Boys prefer buddies who don't require much more than exercise and protein. Sleek coats and sinewy bodies describe the top choice for these testosterone-pumping builder-uppers. The Bull Terrier heads the list with his true enjoyment of physical activity and his fun personality. The Bull Terrier likes to be involved in his owner's routine, so this bulgy gladiator can be walking the treadmill right alongside his well-guarded Muscle Mary master. Spare the Bully your spin class, as dogs don't spin as well as toned gay boys. The Boxer, an athlete in name and at heart, boasts one of the best bods in dogdom: "His well-developed muscles are clean, hard, and appear smooth under taut skin," according to the AKC standard. Although flat faced, the Boxer lays claim to great endurance, stamina, and energy; a well-bred, well-conditioned Boxer enjoys a good cardio workout as much as any pumped gym bunny. Likewise, the Boxer's hindquarters are as well muscled as that of his obsessive butt-sculpting buddy. This German workout partner will serve as a lifelong friend who will spot you without fail.

The Doberman Pinscher makes an unswerving companion and guard dog. He is as sweet and biddable as he is powerful. He's a lot of dog and requires an owner who's available and dog smart. Equally handsome and built like a Falcon model is the Giant Schnauzer, one of the hardest and manliest of all dogs. This is a healthy working dog who only requires his owner to keep his hard, thick coat groomed. Schnauzers need to be groomed to look like Schnauzers—without the beard and furnishings, all you have is an ugly, brawny, giant Poodle!

For easy-care sporty dogs, consider the Airedale Terrier, the German Shepherd Dog, the Weimaraner, and the Whippet. The Airedale and Whippet fit ideally into smaller living spaces, and either one would be the perfect accessory for a Chelsea or WeHo gymrat. The GSD and Weim, both larger and more active, are also adaptable and devoted companions who like lots of activity.

Naturally, gay power lifters have an affinity for the marines—and who can blame them?—for what lies beneath that stiff white uniform is the brawny body of a Bulldog. The official mascot of the U.S. Marines (and those bright boys at Yale, too), the Bulldog remains an irresistible choice for this tribe. Not athletic like its American Bulldog counterpart, the traditional English Bulldog is a pet and not a running partner. Even so, he's a worthy canine who's bound to attract off-duty marines and unreserved reservists to follow you home.

SHOW TUNE & OPERA QUEENS

Drama queens, aptly crowned for their sensibilities and affinity for the stage, require a dog with flair, presence, and that elusive *je ne sais quoi*. Show Tune and Opera Queens are *gay* in every sense of the word, and their gayness exalts their every mood and moment. Only the gayest of dogs will make the cast.

The Afghan Hound is peerless for her commanding presence and innately dramatic ways. That long-haired Bohemian is followed by the Standard Poodle, without a doubt the world's greatest show dog. Poodles have an innate sense of the fabulous. Of course, Bernadette Peters, the first lady of the American musical theater, owned a Poodle: "Both have big eyes, fluffy hair, and a limited vocabulary," quipped Ellen Stein in *New York* magazine during the previews of *Mack and Mabel* in 1964.

Drama queens demand the unique, and the Chinese Crested, with her tufted head and tail—not to mention her fabulous furry go-go boots—would make any queen surrender her blow dryer. It doesn't hurt that Gypsy Rose Lee kept a colony of these dogs either! Show queens cannot resist that straggly little dog that followed Judy around in the great biblical epic *The Wizard of Oz*. That supporting actress was a Cairn Terrier (and you can name yours Toto Two). The Cairn is a stubborn, tough as nails dog that needs a strong, loving man in his life to keep him balanced—just like Judy herself.

Pearl-clutching Opera Queens exalt in breeds that exude high drama: the Shiba Inu, with the demands of a major diva and the voice of David Daniels; the Pharaoh Hound, an Egyptian god for the Opera Queen with allergies (name her Aida); the Yorkshire Terrier, a diminutive bundle of blue and tan silk that's owned by La Voigt (she calls hers Steinway); the Chow Chow, the Chinese empress who scowls at any queen who doesn't "get" opera; the Papillon, for her unmistakable air of self-importance and those fabulous feathery ears (name her Butterfly); and the Norwegian Elkhound, ideal for those incurable Wagnerians who love them loud and long (name her Birgitte). Among this cast list of dramatic canines are dogs of the spitz variety with a tendency to stray, not unlike Show Tune Queens themselves, always looking for the next exciting opening.

Show Tune Queens have varying criteria for their breeds. Raised by eunuchs and other distinguished gay men, the Pekingese effortlessly commands center stage and is the most frequently cited breed in the lyrics of Cole Porter ("Love Me, Love My Pekinese," being a personal favorite*). Show Tune Queens adore the Boston Terrier, like the American musical theater itself, for his wherewithal, showmanship, and originality—this is one that previewed in Boston and has been running ever since. The Finnish Spitz is revered in the dog world for his voice; in Finland the breed competes vocally in the show ring and can even out-yodel Julie Andrews. Oddly, the Mexican Hairless has captured many Show Tune Queens' hearts, possibly for its unexcelled vivacious spirit, its uniqueness, and its uncanny resemblance to Patti Lupone in profile.

**Footnote: For unknown reasons, Porter intentionally misspelled "Pekingese" in this title, omitting the "g." The author, being a Show Tune Queen in therapy, consulted every known source, including* The Complete Lyrics of Cole Porter, *the published sheet music, and the Ben Bagley recording to confirm this unusual spelling.*

SIZE QUEEN

What's in a name? What does your royalty demand? In the Size Queen's world, more is always more! Bigger is better, in every respect. You drive a big car. You live in a large house. You live large and you want a dog (and a man) who can measure up. If it's inches you're counting, look up to the Irish Wolfhound, the world's tallest dog; if it's pounds you're counting, the Mastiff is the world's heaviest dog. Just because a dog is large doesn't mean he's going to last longer, and this is the sad truth with both of these loving giants. Both breeds do not live more than ten years, which in dog years is about seventy, and in gay years, about twenty. Thus, a giant makes a decent long-term relationship, but not a very long-lived canine companion. The Bullmastiff is a bit smaller than the Mastiff and, if acquired from reputable sources, outlives his giant cousin. The Great Dane, long hailed as the Apollo of Dogs, impresses even the greediest Size Queen with his manly grandeur and girth. Big-dog lover and an Apollo in his own right, gay Olympian Greg Louganis dives to mind when thinking of loyal lovers of the Dane.

Now let's move on to the Standard Dachshund: this is the largest weiner dog in the world. He loves to be cuddled and petted, he's a fearless hunter and watchdog, and he's 100 percent German. In the fatherland, Dachshunds are measured by their girth and not their height (or length).

For the Size Queen who's looking to attract a man who's going to live up to every expectation, you might consider one of these breeds. The Italian Greyhound is a sleek, elegant home companion, graceful and intelligent—the perfect choice to strike up conversations with Mediterranean guys in the park. More adventurous Size Queens might consider the Rottweiler, the American Staffordshire Terrier, or the American Pit Bull Terrier, as all three of these handsome canines will catch the eye of Chocolate Daddies about town. If you're playing your odds (and you obviously are), the Bully type dogs are hands down the Homothug's favorite dog. You're sure to impress him, but consider also that your Pit Bull may not get along with his, so renting one might be the better option. There's always a Pit Bull at the local animal shelter: volunteer as a weekend dog walker!

BOY
TOY

SOUTHERN BELLE

Sunny young men, buxom boys, and sweet-talking gentlemen heat up the Deep Gay South. Every polite and good-looking gay man whose drawl betrays him qualifies as a Southern Belle. Admittedly, some are ringers and others rung. Real rebel queers ain't much into *faincy* dogs. The South has long been the land of the hound dog. Southern sportsmen swear by their virile hunting dogs, although most southern gay boys aren't out to bag a raccoon on a Saturday night hunt. Reckon any coonhound worth his grub could track a wily college boy at Hotlanta? The Bluetick Coonhound is the true Mardi Gras hound: his origins, like those of the famous Quarter, derive from the French, and his handsome face is perfectly framed by rainbow-colored beads.

For Southern Belles seeking a simple, slow-moving companion, the Basset Hound voices his vote. He's good natured, polite, and low slung, just like a well-endowed Tennessee princess. The scenthounds remain a mainstay in the South, and lots of gay ole country boys grew up with Beagles and other foxhounds. Don't give any foxhound too much freedom, or he'll be following his nose to the Mason-Dixon Line.

There's no doubt that rebel gays have taken a stiff liking to the American Pit Bull Terrier and the Rottweiler. Like real Southern Belles, these dogs need to be treated right. Train them well and teach them manners, as these are two volatile dogs when mistreated or irresponsibly trained. You've not seen anything until you've seen a Rottie with a bad temperament: he's pissier than a color-blind Drag Queen shut out of the Purple Party on a warm May night.

For the Union Jacqueline looking for a versatile companion who likes outdoor fun, the English Pointer is the best partner east of the Mississippi. Not only is the Pointer a hard man's hunting dog, but he's also no frills, good looking, and gentlemanly. For southern gay gents who like it on the go, the Longhaired Whippet—a rebel himself—is the breed of choice. Although legit Whippet breeders shun the "longhairs," these Silken Windhounds are undeniably elegant and beautiful with their lustrous, long, and silky coats blowing in the warm Dallas breeze.

The sporting and hound breeds won't ripen the interest of a Georgia Peach looking for a smaller, even fancy, playmate. There's nothing the matter with a pal you can keep in your pocket or fanny bag. In the spirit of the ever-popular Fox Terriers, the tiny Toy Fox Terrier is the top choice for the queer royalty of Tara. The most irresistible four inches a queen's ever palmed, the TFT has miles of personality and more opinions than a redneck on a soapbox on Election Day. Two other delightful darlins', adored by Dixie chicks and tricks alike, are the Yorkshire Terrier and the Chihuahua. Both of these can fit into your hand (bag), but don't let that fool you. With any toy dog, you're strongly advised to train them well if you don't want them running the plantation their way.

For Southern Belles looking to hitch a ride with a rugged gentleman caller, invest in the Catahoula Leopard Dog, the state dog of Louisiana. This fearless, manly man's dog will get any southern boy's heart racing: it's the one breed that's sure to make the South rise again and again.

TWINK

Youth fleets like a Whippet in the wind, no matter how firmly the Twink holds on. Nothing warms a queer man's heart more than a Twink in puppy love or fierce running shorts. Twinks come in a variety of flavors, although they're mostly sweet. Twinks can take the form of Pixies, Powderpuffs, and Party Boys, thus a wide variety of purebred dogs appeal to the members of this category.

Pixies tend to be flighty and noncommittal, not very athletic, and endearingly vain. The dog of choice for this lacy Twink is the Miniature Pinscher. Few breeds are as easy care, easygoing, and like all Twinks, just easy. The MinPin, known as the King of Toys, would give this queen something less fleeting to wake up to. Other delish daffodil options are the Cairn Terrier, the Lakeland Terrier, and the Welsh Terrier, although these close-bonding mates require trips to the grooming salon and an owner who's consistent in training. All three of these terrier breeds are small enough to pick up and carry when you need to make a run for it.

The Powderpuff Twinks are well-oiled "debutramps" who don't belong to gyms and aren't nocturnal like the Party Boy Twinks. They would do well with a dog that likes to be pampered and primped such as the Pomeranian and the Shih Tzu. Both of these toy breeds bond closely with their owners and enjoy quiet time at home. Other terrific breeds to consider are the fun-loving Affenpinscher and the Cavalier King Charles Spaniel, both elegant little dogs who like civilized society and limited exercise.

The Party Boy Twink is the most elusive and evasive of the tribe: he rarely returns phone calls, has few friends he can rely upon, and lives for the next circuit weekend. Whether he's in all white or all black, this Twink is colored "gone." If he's going to commit to a four-legged companion, he needs a dog who is emotionally available and truly devoted. First on the list is the Yorkshire Terrier, a nearly human baby of a dog who will live for his daddy and never pass judgment, even when daddy comes home black and blue from the Fireball or Fantasy Fest. Known for their sweet temperaments and kindhearted natures, the Cocker Spaniel and the Shetland Sheepdog make ideal, loving companions. As long as this Twink has a job and can afford a grooming salon, both the Cocker and the Sheltie are manageable and will adapt to your nocturnal schedule. They are easy to train and happy to share their knowledge of the world. From either of these two canines the wayward "dilettwink" will learn some much-needed life lessons: come when called, sleep in your own bed, leave with the one who brought you, and don't let a stranger dock your tail.

TWO-SPIRITS

No portrait of the American landscape is complete without its natives. Apache, Aztec, Cherokee, Cheyenne, Comanche, Navajo, Pueblo, Sioux—about 800 tribes make up the Native American community on the continent. Not every tribe embraces its Two-Spirits members, a term referring to these gay men's equally developed masculine and feminine sides. Many moons before homophobia was injected into Indian culture by missionaries and other collared white-faced men, the Two-Spirits were revered as a third sex, with special healing and counseling abilities. Indians valued these unique men for their talents, not judging them for their sexual practices. While Two-Spirits haven't yet conquered Hollywood the way gay Cowboys have, they have come out yelling *"Jeronhomo!"* It's no surprise when you think that one of the original Fab Five wore an American Indian headdress: Felipe Rose of the Village People is Lakota Sioux by birth.

Many accounts reveal that American Indians have long shared their homes with dogs of various types, mostly midsize pariah- or spitz-type dogs, who assisted them in hunting and other such tasks. The breed most like these ancient dogs is the Carolina Dog, the state dog of North Carolina, the territory where the Cherokee tribes and other Native Americans still dwell. Although a rare breed by most counts, the Carolina Dog continues to be bred and promoted in the United States.

The Mexican Hairless, known as the Xoloitzcuintli (pronounced "show-low-eats-QUEEN-tlee)," was bred by Aztec Indians and certainly is a unique, if not particularly attractive, canine. No longer a delicacy, the Xolo enjoys being invited to the table as a guest instead of a main course.

Modern Two-Spirits gays would admire any of the spitz breeds of Japan, especially the giant Akita, whose intensity and unquestionable nobility would capture the heart of any gay young brave. More akin to the Carolina Dog, the Basenji, originally from the Congo, also offers its unique brand of intelligence and mystical presence. Similarly, the Rhodesian Ridgeback, from Africa as well, proves a dynamic, powerful coursing dog who likes to be by his master's side day and night.

Other outstanding options for Two-Spirits on the move are the Pointer and the Brittany, both refined hunting dogs with long histories in America. While the Pointer remains similar to its foundation stock in England, the American version of the Brittany is a wholly different breed from its French forebears. Colored in orange or liver, the American Brittany is a stylish, longer coated sporting dog who looks sharp on the end of a rainbow leash.

Like proud Two-Spirits people, the sighthound breeds are complex, multidimensional creatures. Strong running breeds such as the Saluki, the Whippet, and the Greyhound are lithe, tireless athletes who possess sensitive, aloof natures and God-given awareness of their elegance and "feminine" mystique.

YENTA

Oi vay! The shadchan arrives today with the perfect puppy for every gay Jewish boy in the village—Greenwich Village, that is—and she's a real doggy *maven* of a matchmaker. For the gay Jewish princess who's *frum* (that's a strict Orthodox Jew who won't pet a dog on Shabbat), let's begin with our only Jewish breed, Kelef K'naani, the Canaan Dog, the national dog of Israel. Here's a versatile, bright, and somewhat demanding overachiever, like every premed and prelaw Jew schooling in the Ivy League. The *New York Times* would give up those shunned Irish fags from the St. Paddy's Day Parade if twenty Jewish queens from Queens would crash the Israeli Day Parade with a dancing pack of Canaan Dogs—the K-9 Klezmatiks, perhaps.

Although any sweet Jewish faggola would love a Canaan Dog, most will choose a goy breed, just like their goy boyfriends. The shadchan's match for the fun-loving *bokher* would be the Golden Retriever and the Collie: both love to be on the go and involved in their owners' busy lives. For the tough *parshoin* with class, better you should choose the Boxer, a medium-size active breed that thrives in the city and the 'burbs. Likewise, the Bouvier des Flandres may also appeal to the outdoorsy Jewish boy, although this bearded herding dog more likely belongs with a Klezbian.

For nice refined Jewish boys looking for affectionate dogs to fit into their city apartments, the perfect *shiddach* should be a Pomeranian, an Affenpinscher, or a Brussels Griffon. Each of these irresistible *tsatskehs* needs a sensible, responsible owner. *Grobers* need not apply.

Another favorite doggala comes in the Frenchie—no *billik pisher!* If you're a *foiler* and are unafraid to let go of some serious *gelt,* the French Bulldog's price tag won't make you *plotz.* He's a pricey purebred, so don't kvetch over the price tag.

For dogs with real chutzpah, we look to the terriers—the Scottish Terrier, the West Highland White Terrier, the Wire Fox Terrier are down to earth yet cocky, confident, and carefree. All terriers are self-reliant, full of themselves, and gaily courageous.

For the *shiksah* faggalas and the rest of the gay goyim who are going *meshuga* from all of this Yiddish, I leave you with this ancient adage, sung by the divine duo of Streisand and Summers and adopted by disco queens from Jerusalem to Boca Raton: *Genug iz genug!* "Enough is enough!"

AND PUPPY MAKES THREE

How many times have you heard your rum-ridden great aunt exclaim at the holiday dinner table, "You silly fags have nothing in common except those damn Pekes!"?

Or, worse, when your partner's mother announces to visitors, "If these boys didn't have ten Lhasas to groom, they'd have some time for a sex life!" Straight people don't quite understand. Nothing holds a gay couple together better than the mutual love of a purebred dog. Just as straight couples stay together until the kids graduate high school, gay couples stay together for the life of their first dog, or second dog, or until they've put championship titles on every puppy in a single litter. Most of the prominent gay men who show dogs today are in supportive, long-standing relationships. The author interviewed dozens of such couples, and many of them emphasized how much their chosen breed of dog enhanced and strengthened their commitment to one another.

Men in long-term relationships usually consider their four-pawed family members to be as important as the biped members. The commitment to the dog's well-being reaffirms each partner's dedication to the other. Gay men don't abandon dogs because they're downsizing their home or moving to another state.

For gay men living in a dogless marriage, a four-legged third can really spice up the relationship. A well-chosen, well-bred dog can add a component to the relationship that may be missing. A puppy can ignite a couple's parenting instincts and add warmth and excitement to the home. Remember, however, that the patter of four little feet is also accompanied by piddle and piles, so don't be too hasty in the decision to bring in a third who's going to stay for ten to fifteen years. For many couples, an occasional third is a good thing, but courteous thirds usually leave voluntarily after coffee.

fab

GAY ADOPTION RIGHTS AND WRONGS

Many factors come into play when opting for adopting, whether it's a puppy or an adult dog. It's no less complicated—in fact it can be more so—for a couple to choose a breed than it is for an individual. Every gay man has a highly individual sense of what is aesthetically pleasing, fashionable, and suitable, not to mention livable. Guys who are titillated by the unattainable and the impossibly buff may perceive an aloof but beautiful breed such as the Chow Chow as their ideal. For gay men fantasizing about adopting a baby, a flat-faced, round-eyed, and round-headed breed such as the Pug, the English Toy Spaniel, or the French Bulldog may fill the empty bassinet. Others prefer the long and lanky and see great beauty in a slender and elegant sighthound such as the Saluki. The majority of gay men take a collective sigh in the presence of a long-locked demigod in the form of a Maltese, a Shih Tzu, or a Yorkshire Terrier. Beauty is indeed in the eye of the beholder.

> "If you have a partner, you will need two dogs—just in case you come home one day and find him in bed with someone other than the 'Monkey Terrier.' You can keep one, and the philanderer can have one in the divorce settlement."
>
> —Jerome Cushman, Hilane Affenpinschers

For some couples, the breed of choice may be a mutual impulse, perhaps sparked by an irresistible Brussels Griffon puppy they met in the park—so ugly he's cute—or a playful Golden Retriever in the neighbor's yard who barks "hello." Adopting a dog may be a much-talked-about fantasy for the couple, although both have been afraid of the commitment of parenting a pair of Poodles. If there's no dream Cocker in the couple's mind's eye, it's going to take some homework and heart searching to come up with the dog who fits the couple like a glass slipper.

Couples should begin by making a list of the things they have in common. Such a list should include such areas as activities, hobbies, favorite vacation spots, and weekend outings. Assuming such a list is possible and some of the entries involve clothing, consider how a dog would fit into your lives. Given the whole wide world of dogs, there's a breed that can fit into every lifestyle, from the active outdoorsy Bear to the stay-at-Homemaker. There's a dog for you whether you're mountain biking on weekends or sitting home rereading eight volumes of Proust.

Next each partner should make a list of what he is looking for in his potential pet. The list should include such items as the size of the dog, the level of activity, the level of maintenance, the length of hair or the amount of coat, the temperament, the abilities, and the trainability. With any luck, there are some similarities between the two lists. In the worst-case scenario, which is more likely than not in some queer pairings, one guy is thinking sweet, fluffy lapdog with a button nose, and the other is thinking 200-pound guard dog with big paws and a wiry coat. Compromise is always the name of the game, although the one who is going to train, walk, and feed the dog should have the home-court advantage.

For couples who simply can't agree on a breed—when even a stack of sex coupons has failed to land the Maltese puppy—there is another option. It's time to don the Mother Teresa costumes and take a drive to the local shelter. There's nothing gay about a mutt, but there's also nothing more American! For this once, we'll run Old Glory up the flagpole and put the rainbow at half-mast. To the outside world, rescuing a mongrel from a shelter appears virtuous and altruistic. Hide behind that noble badge of honor, and never admit to your friends that you just couldn't convince your Cowboy husband that a Bichon was a great sidesaddle pooch. "We just felt compelled to save this little mutt that some selfish straight guy abandoned so he could buy his kids a Labradoodle."

The home also has an impact on the adoption and selection of a dog. If you live in the suburbs with a fenced yard, you can accommodate almost any dog your heart desires. If you are city dwellers, living in a small apartment with limited access to the outdoors, certain breeds, such as that giant wire-coated guard dog, would be much more challenging to own. Small breeds and less-active breeds adapt better to the paved world of the city. Ideally, it's best to leave the large working breeds, including the hunting dogs, herding dogs, and guard dogs, to suburban and country lives.

Married with Chihuahuas

Gay unions are as volatile as straight ones. Statistics show that over half of the "legal" marriages in the country end in divorce, bitterness, and great expense, although many marriages are "saved" by the couples' offspring. Dogs don't fare as well as the kids, and humane-society reports reveal that a fair number of dogs are abandoned every year by bitter divorcées. Perhaps gay couples really regard the dogs as the "kids" and are more likely to stay together for the Chihuahuas.

Gay couples who have "gone to the dogs"—those who are "in" the dog sport—often rely on the dogs for their fulfillment, income, and well-being. These dog families are documented through multi-generational pedigrees and recognizable kennel names. One partner in the dog-world power couple is the breeder and kennel manager, and the other is the groomer and exhibitor; sometimes one is the breeder and the other is the business manager. While straight men establish families, gay men establish kennels or lines of dogs, and coupled gays in the dog world truly live for their dogs, their breed, and sometimes each other, too.

With that said, registration statistics show that Labradors, Goldens, and German Shepherds rank in the top five breeds for most of the big cities in the United States, attesting to the adaptability of these popular companion dogs (and the lack of originality of most metro heteros). Most dogs—given attention, exercise, and responsible care—will adapt happily to their owners' living situations. However, hardcore working dogs, such as the Border Collie, the German Shorthaired Pointer, and the Siberian Husky, usually prove unhappy residents of a Chelsea or Capitol Hill apartment (although not always). For suburbanettes who have chosen their communities wisely, you have the advantage of a good doggy school system, a reliable doggy day care center or boarding kennel, and good veterinary practices and emergency clinics. You live in canine Camelot, and no tax dollars have been squandered for any of these commodities. Three cheers for the GOP!

Of course, both partners must be willing to invest the time into training and caring for a dog, which usually means "making time." If one partner is home during the day or can stop at home at lunchtime to let the puppy out, the training will progress on schedule. Some careers and schedules simply do not allow such luxury. The services of doggy day care and dog walkers may be a solution for dog-owning working couples.

Consider as well that social obligations can be hindered by owning a dog. It is not as easy to stay out all night or hotel it when there's an expectant dog at home with a full bladder. Weekend getaways require a dog sitter or a dog-friendly locale.

Remember that dogs are a financial commitment. The initial cost of the puppy is a mere down payment when you consider the annual cost of food, veterinary care, accessories, boarding, day care, grooming, and other essentials. If your puppy is going to be a show dog, there's another whole spreadsheet of expenses to consider, including trainers, handlers, groomers, travel, hotel bills, and advertisements.

WHY FOUR PAWS ARE BETTER THAN TWO

Many gay men (and lesbians, for that matter) have taken the "family" terminology to the heterosexual extreme and have adopted (or begun the process of adopting) babies. Adopting human babies is a lot more complicated than purchasing a puppy, no matter how rare the breed or exclusive the lineage. The trip to Beijing or Guatemala alone (not to mention all those bribes) can really deflate your Hermès handbag.

Most gay couples, however, fall into the DINK category, which according to gay author and sex-advice columnist Dan Savage means "Double Income No Kids." They aren't into having their own two-footed human baby because infants tend to make a major dent in one's circuit schedule and force gay men to grow up and stop acting twenty-three. Besides, puppies are more fun, less work, and much cheaper. Even the campaign of a top show dog isn't as costly as six years at Harvard! And with puppies you don't have to worry about their coming home with body piercings, herpes, or gangster rap CDs.

A BITCH IN YOUR BED

To bed or not to bed, that is the question. Once little Brandon promises not to pee in your bed, the temptation not to crate him at night is a cozy one. For your lonely gay heart, bonding with your Superpuppy on your Sealy spells real doggy companionship. In dogspeak, sleeping in the master's bed spells equality. The master decides where the puppy is to sleep as well as when the puppy eats, drinks, plays, and even pees. Your alpha-dog role extends to the bed, and sharing it can lead to complications, including aggression, lack of discipline, and pee stains on your 1,000-thread-count sheets.

When your singledom is interrupted by a bitch in heat—that is, a boyfriend who's ready to stake his claim for a side of the bed—adolescent Brandon will be most unhappy to give up his Egyptian-cotton real estate. To avoid having to choose between your dog and your bitch, don't start the puppy on the bed. Place his own bed (or crate) next to yours, and encourage him to sleep there. He just wants to be near you—he doesn't need to be on top of you or sharing your pillow.

If it's too late and you're already in the middle of a blanket-hogging contest with your two loves, you have to evaluate what's at stake here. Cuddling with daddy is a privilege for a dog when he's behaved. It has to be earned. If your well-behaved boyfriend is willing to share the bed, then he's a keeper. As much as we all love our dogs, we must admit that dogs *never* share. They are greedy and self-centered by nature, especially when food, marrow bones, and pillows are concerned. A viable compromise might be to allow the dog on the bed every third night, if your boyfriend concedes, and on the other two nights give the dog a special treat or his favorite bone right before you close the door to enjoy yours.

A MAJOR FABULOUS PURCHASE

Buying a puppy is the grand dame of shopping experiences. You are not headed to the outlet mall with your AmEx card. Why start buying off the rack now?!

Surely, the new puppy is as important as your pride ensemble or your sister's wedding dress. Your puppy is a special-order item. You're looking for top-shelf haute couture, and you can't find it in a department store at the mall—not even a Beagle from the pet boutique at Harrods comes with the proper accreditation.

Don't be afraid to be a snob's snob like the great aristocratic Cole Porter, who didn't believe himself to be a snob just because he preferred the best of *everything.* When it comes to your canine best friend (and your human friends), insist on the best. It's what separates gay men from plebeians and hookers.

Pet shops sell wonderful doggy accessories but strictly pet-quality puppies. Cute, granted, but not fabulous or the reserve vintage. Gay men never settle for the ordinary (or less than ordinary). Pet shops sell the Canal Street version of the purebred dog you want. Now you know that the Maltese behind the smudgy glass is actually a cheap vinyl Kate Spade look-alike. In fact, if you study your breed and look over its standard, that button-nosed beige puppy is likely a sad imitation. Do not bargain shop, as you'll pay more in the end. *Imagine* paying full price for Armani alligator slip-ons only to realize, once you get them home, that they're molded plastic! Hell hath no fury like a queen ripped off on Rodeo Drive!

CHEAP JOE'S
"Almost the real thing – just cheaper!"
CHANNEL
CHANNEL
CHANNEL
CHANNEL
BLURBERRY
BLURBERRY
BLURBERRY

Pet shop dogs come from commercial breeders and small hobby breeders who don't associate themselves with parent clubs. That is because a reputable breeder—one accredited by his breed's parent club—signs a Code of Ethics with his parent club that forbids him *ever* selling a puppy to a third party. Commercial breeders produce dozen of breeds (and, lately, crossbreeds) in volume. If it's white, smallish, and long-haired, they call it a "Maltese"; if it's tricolored, medium size, and long eared, they tag it a "Beagle." Forget breed type, breed standards, and most important, health—it's about sales and turnover.

Commercial breeders have to ship their livestock from one of our otherwise friendly midwestern states—halfway across the country from most of us queers living by the bay, the river, or the ocean. Pet shops need to peddle puppies when they're at their button-nosed cutest, which is seven to eight weeks of age. To get that half-baked Pekingese into the front window, the puppy has to be whisked away from her mother at five weeks of age, about four or five weeks too soon. Such puppies are not properly weaned or socialized and are compromised in health, development, and social skills. Drab mall retailers with no interest in purebred dogs or their customers do not make for pleasant shopping experiences.

At the risk of losing book sales to my gay Amish fan base, a number of the Pennsylvania Dutch folk have become notorious for raising puppies under farmlike conditions and selling directly to brokers. Their dog-proud German relatives would be appalled; the Amish should stick to what they're best at: quilts, pretzels, and high fashion.

Another recent trend involves the importation of puppies from overseas commercial breeders, largely from less privileged countries in eastern Europe and Central and South America. U.S. government regulations are even less restrictive of these imports, further enabling puppy dealers to buy low-cost stock of worse quality than the American puppy mill variety. Most of these pups have forged health certificates, fake pedigrees, compromised vaccinations, and poor health. Unsuspecting buyers have no way of knowing that their French Bulldog is actually a Latvian export with a rubber pedigree.

Fashionistas, retail queens, and Guppies know the value of a real label. An authentic Louis Vuitton carry-all duffel will outlast a Canal Street knockoff, and it won't be crippled, blind, or deaf by the time it's two years old. (Louis happily fixes an occasional sticky zipper or torn strap, no questions asked.)

WHO'S AFRAID OF BREEDERS?

Now let's talk about breeders themselves: imagine, if you can, a woofy stud-muffin daddy lifting his six-month-old baby boy out of his stroller. Yes, he's a breeder—just not the breeders we're talking about. Even though those breeders are *not like us,* we all have parents who—at one passionate, unprotected, and/or drunken moment—were.

Breeders (of the dog persuasion) are passionate about their dogs. If you find a breeder who is obsessive, haughty, and control freakish, then you have likely found a great one. Dog people are a different breed of human being, so take this advice: don't let on that you think they're strange. (Some of them really don't know it.) Any person who doesn't love dogs and put his dogs first would be suspect in a breeder's mind. Win the breeder over and play along. Of course you're taking off a month from your Wall Street job to train the puppy to sit! That's why you have vacation time.

How do you know when you've found the right breeder? There is no simple answer to this question. Check to see whether your selected breeder is USDA licensed. Yes, the United States Department of Agriculture grades more than sirloin. (Did you choose a beefy breeder?) You can also call the Better Business Bureau to confirm that there are no complaints filed against him. The AKC can confirm that the breeder is eligible to register the puppies he breeds.

You are looking for a dedicated, experienced breeder, someone who's been "in" the breed for at least ten years and has bred a few generations of his own dogs. Such a breeder has a line of dogs of his own, and you will see the kennel prefix used in the dogs' pedigrees. This is the basis of line-breeding, and most successful breeders practice it.

The breeder is knowledgeable about the breed as well as his own dogs. When you talk to the breeder, you should get the impression that he has his doctorate in Poodles or Pugs. You have met a true dog man (or woman) who eats, sleeps, and breeds French Bulldogs or Boxers. You are in the presence of an otherworldly doggy guru.

The breeder will most likely be a single-breed specialist, although some breeders may raise two breeds. Very few top breeders concentrate on more than two breeds. Trying to master and perfect one breed is a lifetime's work: ask any breeder of a Best in Show dog. Quite commonly, you will find breeders who breed two different terrier breeds or two similar toy dogs. Another possibility is the breeder who breeds a large breed and a small breed or two breeds of the same nationality. For example, many Akita breeders have expanded into Shibas, and breeders of Lhasa Apsos and Tibetan Terriers often are enthusiastic about "all things Tibet." Regardless, you should be able to recognize the breeder's passion, intensity, and unabashed love for his breed. (As I said, the breeder is a kook!)

Avoid breeders who are negative and breeders who "breed pet dogs, not show dogs." No reputable breeder *intentionally* breeds pet-quality puppies. Pets happen. Breeders who denigrate other breeders, judges, the American Kennel Club, and dog shows in general likely have not succeeded in dogs, and they are blaming everyone except themselves. Kennel-blind and plain ole bitter, this breeder will advise you that he doesn't show his dogs because he doesn't *need* some judge's opinion of his dogs, or that every judge is a crook, or that he's not sleeping with a judge to win a class. This breeder has been rejected by judges at shows many times . . . and so have his dogs.

The breeder should be a member of the national parent club and therefore operate under its Code of Ethics. Puppies are never sold younger than seven or eight weeks of age; some breeds are retained until twelve weeks of age. Be wary of a breeder who's eager to sell you any puppy who's five or six weeks of age. A toy-breed puppy should not be less than nine weeks of age. Most clubs include their Codes of Ethics on their Web sites; familiarize yourself with those of your given breed before purchasing a puppy.

As Tina Turner asks over and over, "What's *love* got to do with it?" It's that four-letter word that sells me on a good breeder. You will know when you find a great breeder that the litter was reared with love. That's one ingredient that can't be faked. You can fake cute, frisky, and attentive—we've all been seventeen—but it's the love that seals the deal.

Gays love anything by a good designer, so why not "designer dogs"? The likes of Calvin Klein and Donna Karan are not designing these cute mongrels. Even though Cockapoos have been raised by dear Aunt May since the late 1960s and Labradoodles are almost recognized as a breed in Australia, the designer dogs in the United States present a messy picture. Designer dogs have become "a bad idea gone wrong." Unfortunately, there are so few actual breeders of the designer "breeds," and most aren't breeding to any standard. It sets dog breeding back centuries. No breed standards, no work purpose, no dog shows: anyone can breed a great litter. Take this advice: put on your best Nancy Reagan puss and "Just say no."

Be wary of "specialty" breeders. These are the creative types who are advertising "rare" and "special" versions of recognizable breeds. We're talking about people who are peddling "Teacup and Tiny Toy Poodles," "Miniature Yorkies," and "Pocket Beagles." If the AKC or CKC doesn't recognize the breed, it's probably not a breed. Yes, you can buy a Miniature Poodle and a Toy Fox Terrier, as these are long-standing varieties or breeds. The others are marketing ploys to draw you in. Responsible breeders know that a Yorkshire Terrier can weigh as little as two pounds as an adult—what the hell's a Mini Yorkie going to weigh? Is it a gecko or a dog? At least the breeders selling parti-colored Poodles aren't masquerading their merchandise. You can't disguise a black and white Standard Poodle—here's a harlequin Poodle. You either want it or you don't. (Point of information: Poodles have come in parti-colors for hundreds of years, even though AKC breeders don't like them. These dogs are attractive and should be as healthy as other Poodles. They are great conversation starters in the dog park, too.)

> Is there any doubt that Poodles are the most forgiving of all creatures on the planet? These benevolent animals have allowed us to clipper and shave them, tweeze and tease them, crossbreed them, dye them, dress them in drag, paint their nails, make them march in parades, prance at shows, and dance in circuses. It's a wonder they haven't banded together and gone postal. That's love, baby, real unconditional love!
>
> —Dawne Deeley, Tsarshadow Carelians

WAYS TO FIND A BREEDER

Once you have decided upon the breed of dog, finding a breeder is the next major step. If you've selected a fairly common breed of dog, there should be many breeders in your area. If you've decided upon an ultrachic rare breed, your options are more limited, but your search more straightforward, so to speak.

American Kennel Club. Visit the AKC on the Web (www.akc.org). It is a very useful Web site. Click on "Future Dog Owners," and that will take you to the breeder-referral service. Select the breed, and you will be directed to a national or state breed representative or the national parent club. From there you have phone numbers and e-mail addresses. Follow up e-mails with phone calls.

National Parent Club. You can discover the name of the national club from the AKC Web site; each club has its own Web site or one hosted through the AKC. The Canadian Kennel Club (CKC) site provides club names in Canada. Don't be confused by the term *parent club*: this is the club that protects the breed in the United States and has the AKC's official seal of approval. Examples are the Poodle Club of America, the Golden Retriever Club of America, and the American Pomeranian Club. Each club has a breeder-referral service.

Internet. Not just good for porn, the Internet is a vast resource. Open your favorite search engine, and type in the breed name and "Puppy" or "Breeder." Avoid sites that are general dog or pet sites, as the breeders listed are just advertisers and not necessarily accredited or reputable. Explore the sites that are specific to one breeder. Reputable kennels have phone numbers and street addresses—not just e-mail addresses. If a breeder looks good, check to see if he is a member of the breed club. Don't be too impressed by Web sites with dancing dogs or elaborate visual effects. You're looking for a dog breeder not a webmaster. Some commercial breeders have truly amazing Web sites that are designed to sell their less than amazing dogs. Some of the longest established kennels have very simple, straightforward Web sites. Do *not* purchase your dog online: the Web is for finding information, not buying a puppy (especially not with a recognizable, popular breed). Puppy mills operate online too, and such an establishment will gladly ship you a puppy "before the week is out." Don't buy!

Dog Shows. Here's an essential road trip for any potential dog owner. There are thousands of dog shows every year. Find one within driving distance of your home. The AKC Web site lists upcoming shows, and the sponsoring kennel club usually has a Web site with driving directions and a judging schedule. Meeting the breeders, handlers, and dogs face to face is the best research you can do. Breeders love to meet potential owners at dog shows. Just being at a dog show speaks well of your seriousness in attaining a dog. Breeders are happy you're not shopping for a puppy at the mall or online. Compliment the breeder's dogs and say something sensible about the breed. ("I love their noble bearing." Or, "What a stunning headpiece!")

Talk about the dogs, not about the breeder. Don't overdo it: breeders aren't expecting you to like their clothes or their shoes. Most dog shows are wicked field trips in "what not to wear" (barring most gay men in the ring, of course). Dog-show fashions are fascinating. How else can you time travel to recall what people really were wearing in the late 1980s? Show people spend money on their dogs, not their own wardrobes (unless they're headed into the Group ring at Westminster, and then they run to Herald Square and scour the sale rack at Macy's).

Magazines and Newspapers. Top breeders promote their dogs through advertisements in canine-oriented publications. They display ads in dog-show magazines (such as *Dogs in Review* or *Canine Chronicle*) or kennel ads in *Dog World* or the *AKC Gazette*. On occasion, breeders run ads for litters in a local newspaper, although this isn't very common. Good breeders don't need to rely on classified ads, as usually they have waiting lists for pups. Never trust an ad at face value, regardless of the publication. Puppy buyer, beware.

Shelters and Rescue Groups. Although rarely a source for puppies, shelters and rescue groups often have adult dogs that need a good home. Rescue groups may be all breed (including purebred and mixed-breed dogs) or breed specific, while shelters offer dogs of purebred and mixed lineage. Most rescue groups are run by dedicated volunteers, who keep the good of the dogs in mind. A big commitment and a small donation are all they seek from potential owners.

Veterinarians. Contact a veterinarian in your area to see whether he knows of breeders of your chosen breed. Every breeder relies on a veterinarian, so this is a great way to find out about local breeders. Some breeders post litter announcements in veterinary clinics.

VISITING THE BREEDER

To make an appointment with the breeder, call him on Tuesday, Wednesday, or Thursday. Weekends are consumed by dog shows, and most breeders don't have time for long phone conversations when they're preparing for a show, especially if they have to bathe six Lhasas or groom a litter of Lakeys. Be punctual for your appointment. Visit only one breeder per day.

When you visit the breeder, you should be welcome in his home (or kennel) and permitted to see and visit with all of the dogs. Never deal with a breeder who doesn't allow you to visit with his dogs; you should be able to meet the whole litter. The dam of the litter will most likely be on the premises; ask to meet her. The dam tells you a lot about the way your puppy will grow up. How much have you learned about your lover (or any of your closest girlfriends) by meeting his mother? Just as gay men turn into their mothers, puppies turn into their dams. You

> "Gay men treat their dogs like children, and there are usually no bratty kids around the house to torment the puppy or undo its training."
>
> —Muriel P. Lee, Editor, *JustFrenchies*

may not be able to meet the sire because breeders rent out daddies for stud. What a fabulously gay notion!

The breeder's premises, whether the home or a kennel, should be clean, warm, and friendly. Puppies are poop machines, so don't expect the lobby of the Ritz-Carlton, but the place shouldn't be filthy and stinky. No matter the breed, the puppies should be friendly and alert. Nobody should settle for unfriendly, aggressive, or dim—not even at 2 a.m. when the lights are coming up and you go into panic pick-up mode.

Now brace yourself to be grilled: it's S&M Q&A time. Be warned that breeders are a little sadistic and domineering and don't mind being on top, wearing the spiked collar. First the breeder will ask you about your history with dogs. Have you owned dogs before? How long did you own them? Have you owned the breed before? Why have you selected this breed and this breeder? Do not mention this book! No matter how devoted a Show Tune Queen you are, you'll never be able to convince a Standard Poodle breeder that you need a dreamy black bitch with big hair so that you can call her "Effie."

The breeder will also inquire about your living conditions; your neighborhood; your work schedule; your fence (or lack thereof); your interest in showing, breeding, or competing; if there are any children in the household; and so on. Most breeders are delighted to sell puppies to gay men. Scottish Terrier breeder Muriel P. Lee commented, "The gays make the best puppy buyers. They're ideal dog parents." Although not all breeders are as open-minded as Minneapolis Muriel, most of them keep the well-being of their dogs at heart and do not discriminate. Given the success of gay breeders and exhibitors, most dog people adore "the gays" and consider them ideal customers.

Just like the title to a new car or the Rolex certificate of authenticity, the puppy should come with paperwork. The pedigree should include four or five generations of ancestors. Many of the ancestors will have the same kennel prefix. Look for titles on the dogs' names, the most common one being "Ch." for Champion. If the most recent titles are more than two generations back, they are almost meaningless; it's the first and second generations that you're interested in, the parents and grandparents who should have titles before their names.

The breeder should have a contract that affords rights to both parties. Do not be dissuaded by a breeder who has a formal contract. Breeders have to be businesspeople, too, and the contract protects the puppy first and foremost. The breeder should also have registered the litter with the American Kennel Club (or the Canadian Kennel Club) and provided you with the forms to register your puppy individually.

Most breeders require that pet puppies be spayed or neutered. The breeder will explain the type of registration for which your puppy is eligible. Often breeders stipulate that a pet puppy receive a "limited registration" so that the owner cannot register puppies produced by that dog.

When shopping for a puppy, a breeder's kennel or home is a Rodeo Drive boutique, a Fifth Avenue designer shop. The last question you ask a breeder is, "How much?" Like shopping at Salvatore Ferragamo for a silk shirt or Manolo Blahnik for pony fur boots, one doesn't fumble around for the price tag (at least not with the cute sales boy watching). Every retail queen knows that if you have to *ask* the price, you can't afford it. A breeder's price should be fair; reputable breeders pride themselves on fair dealings. The price tag will reflect the breeder's superior stock and expertise. Quality is recognizable and always appreciated by people in the know. In fact, you don't need to be a sommelier at the Four Seasons to recognize an excellent glass of Bordeaux nor the first-chair violinist in the New York Philharmonic to know you're at a great concert. With puppies, quality glistens on the outside and resonates from the inside. The puppy is beautiful, with shimmering eyes and coat. He's vital and alert.

Breeders usually charge more for the show-quality puppies in the litter, the ones that are "typey" or "showy." Think of these puppies as "limited editions." There's maybe one or two in every litter; sometimes there is none. Breeders prefer to find homes for their best puppies with owners who intend to show the dogs, and then, if successful, breed them. Pet-quality puppies are usually reserved for owners who want a companion dog. No matter what the breeder tells you, most puppies in the litter are pet quality. Few breeders have ever produced a litter of all champions—even in rare breeds. The term *pet quality* does not indicate that the puppy is inferior in any meaningful way. Usually the pets

Standard Eros

Invest the time to go online and read the breed standard of your selected breed. It's a real crash course in purebred dogs. You'll soon know terms such as *stop*, *hock*, *topline*, and *croup*. Some words that you thought were just bitchy are actually doggy: *cut-up* (smaller waisted) and *dishing* (weaving gait), for instance, have nothing to do with gay small talk. You'll soon be saying things such as "good bone," "giving tongue," and "trailing tail" with nary a giggle. In the show ring, you can even see "hard-driving action" before you're eighteen years of age. And a "Chippendale front" (for once!) is not a good thing, but "low slung" can be very good. You'll even learn that the perfect "otter tail" is thick, round, and tapering! You probably already knew that, but did you know that a "gay tail" is carried above the horizontal level of the back (when the dog is *standing*!)? Have breed standards ever sounded so provocative?

are too big, are mismarked, have slight overbites, lack angulation, and so forth. None of these so-called faults affects the puppy's ability to make a happy, handsome, and healthy companion dog. Even with minor aesthetic drawbacks, the puppy should still resemble the breed in every way. A pet should still possess the key elements that are outlined in the breed standard. There's no sense taking home a Norfolk Terrier puppy that could easily eke by as a Cairn Terrier or an Australian Terrier, or a Beagle who looks more like a Basset, or a Maltese who looks more like a Poodle or a Bichon Frisé. You've selected a breed for the characteristics, both physical and temperamental, of that breed. Don't compromise and bring home a giant yellow Bichon puppy with a nappy wiry coat and the tail of a Westie.

Even if you're not looking for a show dog, you really should read the breed standard of your chosen breed. All of the breeds recognized by one of the registries have a standard, and this written description tells you what the dog's head, body, coat, tail, and other characteristics should look like, as well as how the dog should behave and move. If you didn't read the standard, you wouldn't know that a Shiba Inu is supposed to have small ears that tilt forward. Only when you're in the know will you recognize that those adorable German Shepherd ears are wrong on a Shiba. Likewise, breed standards tell you that a Labrador Retriever shouldn't come in a "rare" silver color or brindle pattern and that a solid-blue Lakeland Terrier is a perfectly acceptable option for the breed.

SELECTING YOUR PUPPY

After an hour or two of phone calls and e-mails, a preliminary interview with the breeder, and a visit to see his home and kennel, it's time to meet the puppies. Perhaps you've already met the mother dog on your first visit, but now she's a proud dam watching over her brood. Depending on the breed of dog, the dam has had two to sixteen puppies. The general rule of whelp is that small dogs have small litters and big dogs have big litters. This is more or less true, but there are exceptions.

Most breeders will have a good idea of which puppy is suitable for which potential buyer. The breeder should know the personality of each puppy in the litter and is experienced with matchmaking. Describe your home life and living environment as blandly and honestly as possible. For this once, don't embellish. Give the breeder a good idea of the lifestyle the puppy will have, including the number of hours you're home, your work schedule, your weekend obligations, celebrities who visit the house, and so forth. Most breeders are delighted to learn that you don't have four Ritalin-charged offspring ready to mangle their eight-week-old puppy the minute he leaves the kennel. Christine Carter is one such breeder:

> I love it when a gay man calls me for a Cairn Terrier or I meet someone gay who is looking for another breed. They are the first to volunteer

plenty of information about their homes and how their dogs live. Often they will send pictures to prove how well they treat their dogs. I hate to make generalizations, but gay men seem to take care of themselves and their homes better than many straights and that usually extends to their pets. A well-groomed man with a neat home is likely to take care of his dog the same way. Naturally, I go through my usual screening process, but I have never turned a gay man or couple down for a puppy while I have to turn away straight people all the time.

When selecting the puppy, you should be looking for a bright, inquisitive dog who is at once alert and friendly. That should describe every puppy in the litter. Do not let the breeder convince you that because the breed standard says the breed should be "aloof," "scowling," "sober," or "reserved," the puppies should be not very friendly. No purebred dog is supposed to be standoffish, suspicious, or untrusting of people. In addition to their bred-for job, all purebred dogs are bred to be companions—Border Collies, Foxhounds, and Greyhounds all have real jobs and yet adore the company of humans.

In any litter, some puppies will be more outgoing and boisterous than their siblings; others may appear shy, retiring, and sleepy. Keep in mind that you can't really judge the temperament and personality of a puppy from a single sixty-minute visit. The laid-back puppy may have been bouncing off the whelping-box walls for an hour before you arrived. The smaller female puppies are likely being harassed by their bigger, bolder male siblings and have taken the back seat just to cope with the boys' sophomoric antics. If possible, you should visit the litter more than once to get comfortable with your choice.

Again, rely upon the breeder's insight and experience to help you select a puppy. Some breeders actually tell you which puppy you can purchase, believing that they know what is best. If you've found a good breeder, then this is a tried-and-true method. Of course, you must share your sex preference with the breeder, if you have one. (Sex preference is different from sexual preference. Unless he asks you, the breeder does not need to know about the first time you knew you were gay. He does not care about your queer revelation while watching Endora or Uncle Arthur on *Bewitched* or about your first locker room experience. The breeder *does* care about whether you prefer a male or a female puppy.)

Male puppies tend to be larger, with more pronounced physical characteristics. The male's head is bigger, his coat is more developed, and his presence is more imposing. As nature intended, males are the beauties of the animal world. Think of the impressively maned African lion, the fantastic peacock, and the achingly perfect Matthew Rush. In canines, the males tend to be more aggressive, more protective, and somewhat more distant. The females, on the other paw, tend to be sweeter, more loving, a bit more finicky, and, of course, moody. (You didn't think gays invented the term *bitchy*, did you? We've merely perfected it.) Each breed (and each dog him- or herself) holds many variations, so nothing is absolute when it comes to the sexes.

Another consideration to discuss with the breeder is color. In some breeds, there's a whole rainbow from which to choose; in others, there's no choice whatsoever. Among the rainbow breeds are the Cocker Spaniel, the Lhasa Apso, the Pekingese, the Pomeranian, the Poodle, and the Shih Tzu. Among the one-color breeds are the Bernese Mountain Dog, the Norwegian Elkhound, the Vizsla, the Weimaraner, and all of the white dogs, from the tall Great Pyrenees to the tiny Maltese. Be sure you check the breed standard for color, as you don't want to buy a "rare" or "exotic" tricolored Dalmatian, a brindle Labrador Retriever, a blue Swissy, or a white Briard. Americans tend to get hung up on color: U.S. breeders frown upon certain colors in certain breeds that occur elsewhere in the world. For example, fawn Schipperkes, white Miniature Schnauzers, and tricolored Brittanys cannot be shown in the United States, but they are widely known elsewhere. At least we can show brindle Basenjis! Of course, color is a nonissue in the hound breeds (such as the Beagle and the Basset Hound) and in all working dogs (such as Border Collies and Pointers).

If you have a color in mind, you should express your preference to the breeder. You may have to wait longer for a café-au-lait Miniature Poodle or a honey Lhasa, but if you're convinced that's the flavor, the hue, and the shade for you, stay the course. With breeds in which there are only three or four options, you may find that certain breeders specialize in certain colors. You can find breeders who concentrate on black Pugs, parti-color Cockers, black and tan Shibas, and silver Miniature Poodles. Don't be too distracted by color, though; it's never a vital factor when choosing a pet. Other factors are more meaningful.

The most important consideration for any puppy is the overall health and soundness.

Unfortunately, most breeds of purebred dogs are predisposed to genetic health problems. Simply put, some breeds are healthier than others. When you are deciding upon the best breed for your lifestyle, you undoubtedly will encounter health information in your research. Many very appealing popular breeds are potential minefields of hereditary problems. German Shepherd Dogs and Golden Retrievers have daunting litanies of potential woes; Miniature Bull Terriers, Bulldogs, and Miniature Schnauzers have fewer but can be equally compromised healthwise if the breeder is not careful.

Responsible breeders screen their breeding stock for potential problems. Hip dysplasia and elbow dysplasia, the two most common orthopedic problems, can be detected through X-rays. Many eye diseases and conditions, such as progressive retinal atrophy, cataracts, and conjunctivitis, can be tested for by an ophthalmologist. Orthopedic records are kept by the Orthopedic Foundation for Animals (OFA) and University of Pennsylvania Hip Improvement Program (PennHIP); eye records are registered with the Canine Eye Registration Foundation (CERF). The breeder should show you the results of these tests as well as health clearances on the litter's parents. A number of other diseases have no genetic markers and can be identified only after the litter is born. In general, the puppy, not unlike a new boyfriend, must be handsome, bright, and well put together.

Now let's discuss the social skills of our intended companion. Puppies, again like boyfriends, aren't born with perfect manners and social grace. The breeder begins the puppy's socialization by introducing the puppy to new people, other dogs, and lots of interesting experiences. By spending some one-on-one time with the puppy, you should be able to determine whether he's a likable, friendly creature. He should respond to your handclapping and your invitations to play. Get down on all fours, and show him what you're made of! The puppy should enjoy your overtures and be more excited than a smack-happy Twink on his first visit to Provincetown. Well, not quite. The puppy you want is enthusiastic, lively, and fun to be around, but not hypercrazy, overbearing, or mouthing everyone he meets (like the aforementioned Twink).

Once you are wholeheartedly positive that you are the right dad for the puppy in your lap, then your mission is complete. A lifetime of responsibility awaits on the other side of the kennel door. Stepping across the threshold is One Giant Step ("Mother, may I?" "Yes, you may!"). Before whirring away into the sunset, be sure you have the contract, the puppy's current health record, the registration and pedigree information, and a feeding schedule. Try to coax a cute friend to come along for the ride so he can hold the puppy (in a towel!) for the trip home. A reliable second choice is a low-maintenance faghag or dog-smart lesbian. Now you're ready to begin family life with your new perfect match.

ENTER THE FAMILY DOG

The only way to survive the arrival of a new puppy is to become a Boy Scout! Be prepared, as the motto goes, although you don't have to dress in that drab uniform and unflattering scarf.

On the day that your puppy is due to arrive, call the bureau and check your credit report. Get your credit lines extended. Call American Express and warn them about an onslaught of activity in the next month or two. Plan to make a large donation to the puppy finishing school of your choice. You and your new charge will become regulars at the doggy boutique in town, the grooming salon, and the canine day spa. There are veterinary visits, health-care insurance, tattoos, and so much more!

You have to shop for puppy essentials: jeweled collars, gourmet treats, juicy designer duds, a canopy bed. Perhaps a summer cottage toward the back of the property. Hire an architect and a meaty builder.

You're preparing a homecoming for the puppy, sending out puppy announcements, catering a puppy shower for 100 of your closest friends, and registering the puppy with the American Kennel Club, Tiffany's, and every boutique in town. You must allot ample time to interview a team of professionals to assist in the care, training, and good manners of your new puppy . . . who has yet to receive a name.

woof!

NAMING YOUR PUPPY

The curse of straightness is being ordinary, blending in with a bland crowd. Gay men "blend" like nuns on a casino floor. In other words, we avoid the "normal" and the "ordinary" . . . well, most of us anyway. One of the most famous show dogs of all time has an exciting gay name: Bang Away! He was a flashy fawn-colored Boxer from the 1940s who became a national celebrity after winning the Westminster Kennel Club Dog Show.

In selecting a name for a puppy, creativity, allusion, and nostalgia light the way. Name your puppy after a Shakespearean character ("Puck," "Hamlet," or "Portia"), opera divas ("Kiri," "Beverly," "Lotte," or "Melba"), or even campy movie actresses ("Bette," "Joan," "Greta," or "Reese"). When in doubt, you can always turn to liquor. "Brandy" has been one of the country's top dog names for decades, but it's too hetero. Reach for a more festive cocktail for your puppy's name: "Cosmo," "Martini," "Gimlet," "Bellini," "Mojito," "Mimosa," or for your new Asian toy puppy, "Mai Tai."

Be true to the breed's personality and nationality: a Chinese puppy needs a fun Chinese-sounding name. A Shar-Pei should be called "Lang" or "Chang," not "Rocky" or "Bruno." Twirl your gay wand and have fun, but do keep in mind that you might one day be shouting the name down Duval Street, so don't go too far. If you have a Chihuahua, for example, you don't want to name him "Rumer," "Scout," or "Tallulah." Let's leave those names for Demi Moore's kids. Actually, Gwyneth Paltrow's firstborn has the perfect Chihuahua name: "Apple"!

In fact, it's been trendy to name dogs after people since the late 1990s. "Max" remains one of the most popular dog names, although gay men would be wise to avoid it. From personal experience (the author's partner named his Vizsla Max before I was there to light the way), it's not becoming to bellow "Max!" through the neighborhood at one in the morning, especially when you sound like an enraged, drunken Norma Desmond. Other common names such as "Lou," "Molly," "Lucy," and "Sam" should be reserved for goldfish and Siamese cats. It could be fanciful to name your puppy after your favorite hot actor, singer, or sports star. Imagine waking up every morning for the next ten to fifteen years to "Welling," "Ricky," "Brad," "Cibrian," "Heath," or "Mario." And that brings us to this thought: "Boner" might seem like a good idea until the day you lose it or lose your dog ("Has anyone seen my Boner"?). Another bad (but funny) choice for your girl puppy is "Mary," but try belting "Mary, come here" at a city dog park and see how many queens pivot and shoot you a bitchy glare.

Be passionate and have fun and soon you'll be standing at the baptismal font with your puppy's godparents. (Of course, if you're a

GAY NAMES AND NONGAY NAMES

TYPE/BREED OF DOG	GAY NAME	NONGAY NAME
Small Dog	CoCo, Daphne, Ginger, Joan, Ki-Ki, Kylie, Lola, Mimi, Sassy, Truffles	Angel, Daisy, Fifi, Jughead, Peanut, Peewee, Precious, Sugar, Taffy
Large Dog	Apollo, Bear, Camille, Norma, Thor, Tristan, Xerxes	Arnold, Attila, Butch, Dubya, Holmes, Jeb, Max, Rambo, Sarge, Tank
Bully Breed	Blanche, Clint, Ethan, Madge, Pierce, Serena, Tab, Topper	Cheney, Gripper, Kid Colt, Mike, Mugsy, Petey, Rocky, Sparky
Scenthound	Bernie, Fred, Garbo, Linus, Magnolia, Tennessee	George, Knuckles, Okra, Rimmer, Ted
Sighthound	Ajax, Co-Jo, Elsa, Maya, Será, Storm, Tryst, Ursula, Venus, Vixen, Zelda	Flash, Nike, Skidder, Spike
Sporting Dog	Hook, Hunter, Keller, Mambo, Marky, Paris, Sarah, Splash, Stump	Bud, Duke, Goldie, Pistol, Sandy, Slinger, Sport, Zeke
Asian Dog	Choo-Choo, Erik, Ginger, Sumi, Suni, Tang, Wasabe, Yahtzee	Ting, Ping, Pong, Pookie, Yang, Ying
British Dog	Delilah, Kate, Oscar, Portia, Puck, Sage, Simon, Victor	Lady, Lassie, Mike, Norm, Oliver
German Dog	Adonis, Dano, Greta, Hans, Lucas, Lulu, Sigmund, Tauskey	Alf, Barney, Duke, Siggy, Sly
Poodle/Bichon	Babs, Bellboy, Diva, Gigi, Hermes, Iris, Mimosa, Moxie, Sammy, Wilfred	Fluffy, Hey-you, Lambchop, Ringo, Silky, Velcro
Terrier	Ashton, Degas, Harry, Hazel, Hillary, Toto, Tricksie	Bandit, Chopper, Fang, Jo-Jo, Rags, Rufus, Scrappy, Yoda

Yenta, you'll be having a nice bris milah for your puppola, whom you'd better be naming after your grandfather's much-lamented Pomeranian.)

THE HOMECOMING

The first piece of equipment you need is a camera! Hire a photographer for the event. Bruce Weber rarely does puppy shoots, and David LaChapelle is too busy, but there are others who do. George Duroy, we hear, shows up with his own lights and the best-looking crew. William Wegman is a huge dog fan and can be lured into your party if the price is right. (And he's lots of fun at cocktail parties.) The goal is to capture every precious puppy moment on film (or in pixels). The days of puppyhood fly by ten times as fast as childhood, so take that many more photos.

Your puppy's homecoming will not be accompanied by floats, twirlers, or a marching band. This is no time for a gay puppy parade. You have to prepare your home for an attack. You are willingly admitting into your home a tiny wolflike creature with a dripping desire to wet on every surface he encounters. He also wants to eat, chew, shred, dig, and destroy everything that moves (and many things that don't move!). Your objective is to protect your belongings and not let your puppy choke to death, impale himself, or get himself crushed under your stuff. Puppies are nearly as fragile as they are destructive.

Puppy proofing relies upon a little knowledge and a lot of surveillance. A puppy in the house is like a crawling infant. Both will put everything he finds into his mouth—in fact, puppies are worse as their mouths are their hands, too. Let common sense be your house guide. If you wouldn't let your two-year-old niece eat a house plant, play in the fireplace, or make pretend love potions with Mr. Clean and Aqua Net, don't let your puppy. Taste testing the contents of ashtrays, licking electrical sockets, and shredding telephone cords are taboo for puppies, too. And, in some ways, it's like de-gaying the house: put away your crocheting gear, sex toys, porn, and makeup case. It's no fun explaining to your neighbors how the puppy got the cover of *Torso* in his mouth. Puppies are more inclined to explore the bathroom and kitchen cabinets—they'll eat your oatmeal and herbal soaps, swallow Brillo pads whole, and make quite a floorshow out of your Trojan party pack. Nail your cabinets shut and close the bathroom door. Puppies also shouldn't be allowed to tour the garage, shed, or pool house. Antifreeze, fertilizers, and pool chemicals kill dogs.

Invest in puppy gates (or baby gates, depending on where you buy them). The high-end ones come in a variety of wood finishes and don't make your house look like a ward. These are temporary fortresses that restrict your puppy from off-limit rooms, such as the

living room, the dining room, and any other room with a priceless Persian carpet, Fabergé trinkets, and chiffon bunting. Puppies don't mean to be Neanderthals; they just don't know the difference between poly blends and Como silk. They learn those niceties in finishing school.

Dog lovers should incorporate their pets' needs into their own homes. It's no longer enough to toss a bed in the corner for the dog to slumber upon—even if the bed is designed by Isaac Mizrahi. A really fabulous gay dog home will be as attractive as it is cozy, for all residents, furry and shaved. Top fashion

A Queenly Sum

You don't have to be a millionaire, or marry one, to raise a puppy in a Trump-like style, but a nice cache of cold cash can certainly improve the situation. The initial cost of the puppy is just the down payment. You are investing in a relationship with more than your heart. This relationship can dent your purse, too. Puppy supplies include, among other items, food, a crate, a bed, toys, training treats, a collar, and a leash. Top-shelf dog food is costly, but it's worth the extra money to know your puppy is getting the right stuff.

Additionally, the cost of veterinary care is beginning to go the way of health care in America, which is to say to hell in a Fendi handbag. Other expenses incurred may include doggy day care, weekly grooming salon and spa visits, boarding or a dog sitter (for vacations without the dog), puppy gates, fencing or kennel runs, grooming supplies, designer clothing, furniture, dishware, obedience schools, and photo shoots. If you make the right decisions about all of the above, your puppy should cost slightly less than freshman year at Bryn Mawr by the time he's ten years of age.

If you're not a Guppy, a high-powered attorney, or a baroness, these expenses may seem daunting. Fortunately, nearly all breeds of gay men are resourceful. Even a party boy on his last bad check has ways of making ends meet, some of which are legal. When in doubt, and a little depressed, do as Judy did: throw a party. But first register at PetSmart and the puppy boutique in town!

designer Todd Oldham shares, "I designed my apartment to be my dog's home, too. I made sure to design everything to be comfortable for her in every way, so we'd both be happy with the result." In creating such an environment, man and beast cohabitate in a safe, elegant, and seamless home. With any luck, the harmony we feel with our pets and the kindness we share with them will resonate to the larger community. End of sermon. Hymn, anyone?

PUPPY ANNOUCEMENTS

Neither Emily Post nor Miss Manners addresses the etiquette of sending out proper puppy announcements. Fortunately, the author has at his fingertips the longtime personal assistant of Amy Vanderbilt and a popular, albeit straight, dog author, Bardi McLennan. Here's what the "Bard" says about sending canine birth announcements:

> Amy Vanderbilt, the Queen of Etiquette, said a dog has every right to expect his or her new parents to follow this modicum of social etiquette. The birth announcement should include all the vital statistics. And an attractive photo would be a nice addition. Be certain to include the name of the new arrival (followed by call name, if different), date and place of birth, weight, height, color as well as names of the puppy's parents and new adoptive parents.

Michael and Michael
Announce the Arrival of
JustThem's La Bonne Chanel

"CoCo"

A taupe and coffee
French Bulldog puppy
born in the year of the dog
2006, April 14

Through the Expert Midwifery
of Breeder Anita Whelpington

Donations in CoCo's name to the
West Palm SPCA
are sincerely appreciated.

Like proud parents boasting about their firstborn (or thirteenth), couples and individuals can show off their new puppy charges. After choosing the perfect breed, locating a breeder, and picking the perfect puppy from a litter, a gay couple will be elated to share their new bundle of puppy love with their family and friends.

After milking all of your friends for puppy gifts at the shower, you can take a higher road with the puppy announcement card. Consider soliciting donations to the local SPCA or animal shelter in the name of your puppy. If you're not inclined toward charity work (rightly fearful of morphing into a queer Jerry Lewis), you might take your usual underground path and use the puppy to lure some hot acquaintances to your home to meet the puppy and share a glass of wine. Above is a sample of the interior of a puppy announcement.

For exquisite puppy announcements and puppy-shower invites, geared toward the "in" crowd, visit Handsome Devil Press at www.handsomedevilpress.com. You'll feel like a real bohemian with classy stationery to boot.

THE PUPPY SHOWER

Who throws better theme parties than homos? Every gay man knows someone who works at MSLO or who should. Tap into your most creative gay dog-loving friends, and plan a puppy shower. The key to any good gay party is the guest list and the bartender. The shower's theme should revolve around the puppy. If you've adopted a Japanese Chin, a Shiba, or an Akita, for instance, put the puppy in a wicker bassinet and serve sushi and sake martinis. If your new baby is a Boston Terrier or any British terrier breed (they're pretty much all Brits), have a tea party with cucumber sandwiches, dress up like Betsy Ross or Lady Bracknell, and have the bartender dress like a Minuteman or Prince Harry.

Send out puppy-shower invitations! Make them yourself, or order them online from Handsome Devil Press. Be sure the invitation includes all of the essentials about the party, the puppy's name, where you've registered (for gifts, not pedigrees!), and a photograph of the bartender.

For those readers who haven't turned the page, stay here and think about it. Puppy showers not only provide your new baby with lots of gifts but also present a wonderful opportunity for socialization. Be sure to invite fun fags, the apolitical dykes who mingle, and some straight friends, and you'll be certain to clean up. Your puppy will get to experience lots of new smells (Versace and vermouth, for instance) plus meet his first Leatherman and maybe even a sober Drag Queen. Be careful not to invite any scary fags with big hair or those who don't like dogs. You want your puppy's socialization experiences to be positive ones!

Back to the gifts. Make a list of what you need. Be specific so you don't get four nylon harnesses and six crystal kibble bowls. For your clueless dogless friends (or the Twinks who are coming to see who shows or to meet the bartender), assign them gift certificates to Puppies 'R' Us or Puppy Gap. (Yes, they will try to find those stores. That's why they're Twinks.)

HITTING THE MALL OR THE WEB

Any excuse to forge ahead and charge: nowadays shopping for a new puppy's needs can be as expensive as an off-season weekend in St. Barts. Keeping up with the queer Anderson-Joneses is no easy task. Every gay is walking around with sparkly crystals and a ball of fur! What's a DINK couple to do but spend, spend, spend and support our capricious economic climate? Following are some of the essentials you'll need to keep up with your rainbow-flag-flying neighbors. Remember to post your puppy's wish list online. Register at your doggy boutique or anywhere that sells overpriced canine goods and goodies.

Pet Carriers and Doggy Bags

For guys on the go, a pet carrier is the perfect accessory to your fanny pack or fag bag. These come in various styles, colors, and themes. Of

course, the most upscale of these is the Louis Vuitton pet carrier. Most guys can pull off the backpack or duffle-style carrier, but the bowlers, shoulder bags, and totes will appeal only to guys who are as light on their feet as a Best in Show Maltese. Many of the styles are irresistible, and if you have a soft spot for brass wristlets, the Wonder Woman pet carrier by Modern Tails will have you spinning for days! "Wonder Twin powers: activate!"

Doggy bags are an ideal accessory for guys with portable dogs. Check out the lines by Petote, created by Janet Lee, the first designer diva to devise pet carriers in crocodile, suede, and tweed with leather accents; and PuchiBag, based in West Hollywood, not Florence. The Rio Petote doubles as a roller bag, ideal for taking baby Hugh to Australia (or Rio!) for the weekend. All of these classic leather totes are fashionable, well made, and affordable. Just don't try stuffing a full-grown Sheltie into one. About twenty pounds is the maximum for the large-size tote; ten pounds for the smaller purselike bags. Drag Queens can pull off anything, but other gay men should never succumb to the temptation of stuffing a puppy into a doggy purse. This fashion accessory is a carrier harness devised so that some high-heeled creature can tote her canine tot around like a woman's purse. You know it's Armageddon when gay men start following fashion trends set by the likes of Paris Hilton and Paula Abdul.

It's fairly common nowadays to see puppies being wheeled around town in prams or baby carriages. It's much easier to secure passage into a fine sartorial parlor or even the Taco Bell if your Chinese Crested is tucked away in her carriage. Pet boutiques sell some handsome strollers that are ideal for small dogs and fags unafraid to push them. In a *New York Tribune* article published in 1892, famed American writer Stephen Crane reported on carriages in downtown Asbury Park, New Jersey, observing that "babies and pug dogs furnish most of the victims" inside the strollers. In the same article about the then-proper Methodist city, he reported on seeing a Drag Queen shaking her blues away on the streets: "a terrible creature in an impossible apparel, and with a tambourine." Everything old is new again! Been to Asbury Park lately?

Collar

The appeal of a well-made leather collar cannot be denied, although a basic nylon buckle or snap collar will work on a smaller dog (or drunken frat boy). For training a puppy, a martingale collar (double loop) is more effective, more humane, and safer than a nylon choke collar. The martingale is sometimes also called a greyhound or limited-slip collar. Avoid choke chain collars unless you have a large dog who doesn't respond to any other type of collar or restraining device. Check out the head collars (which fit around the dog's muzzle and neck), as these offer the best control for difficult or strong dogs. Consider as well a halter for a dog who's an escape artist or who resists a conventional collar. Made of nylon or mesh, the halter is equipped with two or three straps that attach over the dog's shoulders and around his torso.

Visit a boutique to see some charming bejeweled and begemmed collars (including genuine Swarovski crystals). Even Hermès has designed a dog collar! Any color, pattern, or design your little gay heart desires can be found, from polka dots, rainbows, and real bow ties to monograms. You can even buy a collar designed by famed Weimaraner photographer William Wegman, not to mention the leather collars sold by Louis Vuitton and Coach.

Leashes

Of course, the leash of choice for any proud gay man is a rainbow leash. Online you can purchase these multicolor nylon leads from many retailers, including www.gaymart.com, www.mygayweb.com, and www.dontpanic.com. You can purchase a collar to match, but that might be overqueering the obvious. The rainbow leash makes an important gay statement: look at my fabulous new puppy and how great my ass looks in these palazzo pants. Other options include a leather leash, which feels better in your hand than nylon. Avoid chain leads as they're heavy, unmanageable, and unmistakably redneck. A retractable leash (a nylon cord inside a plastic case) is excellent for long walks and gives the lead-broken dog more freedom. PuchiBag has sparkly versions of this leash, too, complete with crystals and an eye-popping price tag. You can also purchase collar-and-leash-in-one devices, which are handy for training and showing.

Bowls

Queer husbands of Martha Stewart, of which the author is one, have a pantry full of exquisite dishware ideal for every occasion and gathering. For everyday dining, the Kate Spade dog dish by Lenox will make any Cavalier feel like a queen! For special occasions, consider the Wedgwood dog bowl, designed by Nick Monro for the company's Jasper collection; a fabulous Italian dog bowl by Barocco; or the Spode Blue Italian line. Of course, to be sensible, offer your dog's victuals in fine china only after his *formal* training has been accomplished. No sense bothering with the Spode if your Poodle's going to use the wrong fork!

A terrifically gay alternative to ordinary stainless steel dog bowls are the satin steel bowls, with a luxurious finish and rubber bottoms to keep the bowls from sliding around on the floor. These bowls can be sanitized like ordinary stainless and will better complement your kitchen appliances.

Avoid bowl stands and similar racks for your dog's food. Yes, they look tidy and rather fashionable, but they're bad for the dog's digestion. These bowl stands may be linked to bloat, and bloat is much worse than mild indigestion, which can be nursed by an after-dinner cognac or aperitif. It can be deadly. If you have a deep-chested dog, bloat is always a concern, especially if you don't feed a raw diet.

Crate

For most dog breeds, the crate is an essential piece of furniture. You can even find designer dog crates made out of hardwood, wicker, and rattan to match your drawing room decor. The traditional dog crate is constructed of wire, which most dogs prefer so that they can view their surroundings. (Gay dogs are nosy dogs!) The wire crate comes in hammered pewter or bronze, making the crate easier to accessorize with the hardware in most rooms; some even come in different colors. The airline-style crate (which never looks nice inside the home) is preferred by some dogs who like real privacy (hound breeds, for instance). No one wants a crate that looks like a *crate!* You can purchase a designer exterior to mask these cargo-looking crates. Of course, if you're crating a Great Dane or Wolfhound, just don't have company until the monster is housebroken.

Bed

Nothing says "Spoiled Queer Dog" better than a plush canopy dog bed! Take your time in selecting a throne that matches your prince's or princess's personality. Since puppies chew everything, you don't have to invest in anything too over the top right away. A basic over-stuffed pillow suffices for the young royal. Later you can furnish him with a four-poster bed, a sleigh bed, or a platform bed, possibly made of wicker, bamboo, or rattan. Styles of daybeds, chaises, and love seats range from Grecian to Japanese to Andy Warhol to Rococo Fag. You can even buy a doggy trundle bed or a sleeping bag for camping trips.

Salon Accoutrements

When your Poodle is having a bad hair day, there's no one to blame but yourself. Her hairstyle depends on the quality of the grooming accessories you purchase. Every dog needs different supplies, but a brush and a comb are essential to (almost) every dog. (You shouldn't comb a Komondor, a Puli, or any other corded dog.) The most common brushes are the natural bristle brush and the slicker brush (with rubber or metal bristles). Combs are metal with varying sizes of teeth set at different distances from one another.

For your dog's pedicure and manicure, you'll need a nail clipper (either the guillotine or scissors style) or an electric or battery-operated nail grinder.

A grooming table, available at most pet retail stores, is ideal for most medium and small dogs. Select a table with an adjustable height and an arm and noose (like a leash) to hold the dog still during grooming. Breeds such as Poodles, Bichons, the terriers, and most of the toys require specialized grooming. These coats require electric clippers, stripping knives, different brushes, and professional know-how. If you own one of these high-maintenance breeds, you are well advised to ask the breeder for advice on which grooming tools are best and to get directions to a fabulous salon. Find a stylist you love, and tip her well.

Toys!

No gay home is complete without a toy box! At least you don't have to hide your puppy's toys when company comes. Visiting one of the pet-supply superstores can be overwhelming for a new puppy, but you can make it a positive experience. These pet supermarkets have hundreds of toys, more than even the most destructive puppy can sample. Purchase a variety of toys, made of different materials (rubber, nylon, cloth, rope), so that your puppy has choices. He will likely carry his favorite ones around or sleep with the soft furry ones. Inevitably, no matter how much money daddy spends on the latest interactive dog toy, the puppy will prefer eating cardboard boxes, mangling paper towels, and ripping at anything lacy, stringy, and fringed. Put your panties in a

Real Estate

Investigate building a villa for your canine housemate. Yes, you can contract a doghouse architect to design and build a luxury doghouse or canine condo for Camelot your Cavalier or a doggy duplex for your Dachshund duo Draco and Dylan. Dozens of architects have gone to the dogs. La Petite Maison of Charleston, South Carolina, is among the first to break into this field. Michelle Pollak is the owner and brains behind the company. Doghouses can range from around $5,000 to more than $20,000, and the styles can go from an ornate Victorian or a stately brick Georgian to a classic Craftsman or a Spanish hacienda complete with terra-cotta floors and a tiled roof. Owners may choose to have the dog's house mirror the style of their own dwellings. *This Old House* reported on a Newfoundland named Duke living in a miniature Queen Anne mansion exactly like his owner's home. A doghouse can be furnished and decorated to reflect the owner's taste (or the dog's) and can be completely equipped with lighting, heating, and air-conditioning. A couple of Southern Belles with a clan of six Toy Fox Terriers commissioned a tiny version of Tara, complete with a grand staircase and a flat-screen TV for movie night. A California designer conjured up the House for the Doggie Lama for an austere but tasteful Tibetan Terrier and Chapeaux Château for a Poodle with a penchant for berets and expensive caviar.

higher drawer, and just make sure that the puppy isn't choking on any of the above. The purpose of toys is fun, so as long as the puppy is safe, enjoy the silliness while it lasts.

The influence of designers on dog toys has reached profound heights (or depths). You can purchase a Chewy Vuitton handbag for Camille to mangle, and you can offer Judy electric pink Bark Jacobs to get her back to Oz. Don't deny either bitch a classic black Jimmy Chew, a chic cheetah Manolo Barknik, or a snazzy zebra Dolce & Grrrbana. Check out www.trixieandpeanut.com, www.puplife.com, and www.perpetualkid.com to fill your pooch's designer toy box, closet, and wildest dreams.

As the puppy becomes a dog, you can purchase harder, long-lasting chew toys or share some of your own. There's no predicting which dogs will like which bones. Cowboys insist on rawhide and hooves, and their dogs may like them, too. Hard rubber and nylon bones have their fans, as do Frisbees and those big balls on a rope. Be imaginative, and mix it up.

Canine Couture

Every gay dog at one time or another is asked, "What's in your closet?" Light years past the doggy sweater, the world of canine fashion spans the imagination and is obviously fueled by many dog-wild gay men. In boutiques in small towns and big cities as well as on the Web, you can purchase anything from sensible trench coats and doggy boots to leather vests, harnesses, and camouflage outerwear for your dog. And you wonder why some Leathermen are attracted to small dogs! Doggy couture is not just for Pansies anymore! The Pansies and sister Powderpuffs, however, would be wise to hold on to their platinum cards before filling their closets with their dogs' new clothes. The dog wardrobe extends from cashmere sweaters, Burberry dog coats, holiday dresses, and everyday hoodies to ponchos, suede coats, parkas, kimonos, rainproof jogging suits, overalls, and bejeweled running shoes. As long as there are gay men in the fashion world, there will be a never-ending flow of juicy doggy garments and fashion accessories. Author Cathy Crimmins in her cautiously titled book *How the Homosexuals Saved Civilization* has this to share: "It could be argued that the essence of fashion is gay. Gay designers have influenced every straight woman's fashion choices for the last hundred years."

One such designer, Isaac Mizrahi of the West Village, has recently gone to the dogs, adding small-dog fashions to his line of exquisite women's clothing. As Sandy Robbins reported for MSNBC about the first dog fashion show in New York's Olympus Fashion Week,

> All attention is now focused on the runway entrances, framed to look like doghouses, as a new breed of super-model bounds onto the catwalk to début fashion designer Isaac Mizrahi's newest line of canine haute couture for Target Corp. Amidst howls of delight and wagging tails, the audience is on its feet begging for more.

These comments reveal that canine models are no different from the luscious boys who sashay for Abercrombie & Fitch or Calvin Klein: "There were some temperamental bitches backstage!" Mizrahi, whose hot pink and orange canine polos were all the rage in 2005, clarifies that human fashion and canine fashion are intrinsically linked, with the dogs always a season ahead.

Other big name fashion setters, such as Kenneth Cole, Michael Kors, Dolce & Gabbana, and Gucci, lend their names and labels to the collars and shirts of dogs. Female designers are equally devoted to converting the catwalk to a dogwalk. Such inventive design divas as Nicole Miller, Jill Stuart, Joanna Mastroianni, Kara Kono, and Sherri Stankewitz have introduced collections for the Fido Fashionista. Gooby Pet Fashion even has a naval officer coat that would be a real hit for boys cruising the Pier this spring for Fleet Week. Show a navy boy how much you appreciate his dedication to homo and nation. Studs and stripes forever!

Speaking of decorating, don't forget the bling! Your bitch might require jewelry to complement her stunning apparel. Visit the boutique to see which doggy jewels are available, and be certain you don't confuse daytime jewelry with evening wear.

LE WOOF!
COUTURE
LE WOOF!
COUTURE

Visit www.pamperedpuppy.com, www.glamourdog.com, and www.hautedogboutique.com to glimpse just some of the wonderful world of doggy duds. Remember that clothes make the dog, and with the right ensemble you can transform your Powderpuff into a Powerpuff.

Since rainbow politics are all-inclusive, gay men will want to consider inviting the dogs to their gay wedding. The I See Spot label of Sandy Mahoney and Sharon Bolger of Miami Beach actually includes doggy bridesmaids' outfits and velvet tuxedos for the ushers. Don't forget the pillow for the canine ring bearer. Remember to take lots of photos at the wedding, and send them to your governor and senator.

INSURANCE

Gay puppy parents have some very adult decisions to make. If baby Jake is your first puppy or the first new puppy you've adopted in a decade or more, it may come as some surprise to you that canine health care insurance is a necessary, and not too expensive, evil. Although pet insurance has been around since disco was king, only recently has it become a mainstay of the pet industry. The average expense of two annual veterinary visits won't compel dog owners to invest in pet insurance, but the unforeseen complications down the road can be extremely costly.

Depending on the breed of dog you purchase, the life expectancy can range from eight years to eighteen years. Unfortunately, dogs and humans share many of the same diseases and physical ailments. Among the most common in both species are cancer, cataracts, immune disease, heart problems, and bad hips and knees. With advances in human medicine being mirrored in canine medicine every day, veterinary science

A Day at the Spa

A private club with whirlpools, body wraps, massages, and free-spirited members looking for fun and relaxation—the doggy day spa returns us to the glory days of the baths. The Club on all fours . . . Flex with no leashes . . . it's Steamworks for doggy buddies! All of the pleasure and excitement, minus the steam, sweat, and most of the growling, scratching, and biting. Spas are sprouting up all over the map, and gay dog owners surely relate to the joys of a rejuvenating, leash-free romp with like-minded buddies. Doggy day spas go beyond the bounds of doggy day care, adding shiatsu and aqua massage, hydro- and aromatherapy, hot oil treatments, and many other creature comforts to the mix. Your pooch will be pampered from nose to tail, with a pedicure, conditioning bath, new 'do, and gourmet treats galore. One day spa owner describes the experience as a twelve-hour party at which the dogs "want to hang out with each other, roll around on the floor, lick each other . . . their ultimate version of fun." Why, it is Steamworks after all!

promises longer lives for our dogs; many of the same procedures performed on humans can be used to save, or improve, dogs' lives. From bone marrow transfusions, cataract surgery, and hip replacements to open heart surgery and organ transplants, veterinary science has made some fantastic leaps in the past decade or two.

Of course, these advances in veterinary medicine don't come cheap. Only the spay/neuter clinic gives away free operations; all of these others cost handsomely. Although veterinary hospitals haven't sunk to the depths of human hospitals—charging $100,000 a day for critical care—they will charge you a DINK's monthly salary (or the price of that diamond-studded Rolex) for any one of the procedures mentioned above. Veterinary insurance is worth purchasing when your puppy is but a bundle of fur. Only Donald Trump and the Hilton sisters can afford to not have health insurance. Your veterinarian should be able to provide you with reasonable options: there's about a dozen different companies currently offering pet insurance. Some veterinary specialty facilities even offer their own plans. This way, baby Jake doesn't have to worry about your choosing that Presidential for your next landmark birthday over his new kidney.

HIRING THE TEAM

Raising a canine offspring today is no one-man job. It requires a staff to do properly. Once the puppy arrives home, you should begin scheduling interviews. You should consider hiring as many as ten professionals to assist you in rearing and training baby Paris.

Veterinarian. Arguably, this is the most important person in your pup's life after you and Josh Hartnett. Consider the location of the veterinarian's offices; his policy about making house calls; how polite, efficient, and hot his male vet techs are; and his willingness to fulfill anonymous prescriptions late on Saturday nights.

Beautician. A good groomer is worth his weight in eye glitter. Choose this professional with absolute care as all good homos take their dogs to the groomer weekly for a trim, shape up, or comb out. Take the groomer's knowledge of the breed and its correct appearance into account. You do not want your Dandie to be clipped to look like a Bichon who's been on the rack. If you have adopted a high-maintenance bitch—such as a Poodle, a Bichon, a Wire Fox Terrier, or any other big-haired dog—you need professional assistance to clip her to keep her looking fabulous. A word of advice: if your dog sheds, do not shave her. Nothing may seem as refreshing as a little summer trim, but if it's not involving a single-coated dog or a cabana boy, it's a mistake. Queens who don't know a stripping knife from a cheese knife should make their appointments immediately. Be warned: some groomers travel around in trailers. Avoid these WT pikers. My Shiba wouldn't be caught dead in a "Ghetto Clipper" van! Patronize groomers with fabulous salons that resemble day spas and have cute shampoo boys and lots of overpriced bling.

Nanny. A Yenta would be your first choice, if possible. She will make you feel guilty about abandoning poor Paris (and her) for such long hours every day. She will also overcharge you

Best in Show
VETERINARIAN
BEAUTICIAN
DOG WALKER
HANDLER
POOL BOY

and raise her rates weekly. The second-best choice would be a polite but unattractive Pixie or Twink, less common in the cities but easily located in the suburbs. Be clear about the nanny's responsibilities, including dog sitting, walking, and feeding and enforcing doggy manners. Don't compromise your puppy's first-rate care in hope of nailing a cute but clueless nanny.

Trainer. A qualified trainer with a good knack for canine behavior can help facilitate proper training for your puppy. Attending a class with other dog owners can lead to both educational and social advantages. Be wary of trainers who use rough methods and try to manhandle your puppy even if they have a best-seller and their own TV show. Also, avoid know-it-all trainers. Few people on the planet are more annoying than trainers who think they invented the heel command. If the trainer claims to have famous Hollywood clients or trains stunt dogs for movies, run! For the same hourly rate, you could hire a BelAmi model for the weekend.

Pedicurist. The ever-changing winds of fashion dramatically affect canine pedicure styles. Clipping nails at home is so pedestrian, and it's more fun to pick a nail color with a queen who's certified by Wilfred or Barbizon.

Dog walker. The designated dog walker can be a neighbor, an unemployed friend, or any Lady of Leisure. Alternatively, it can be a single Pump Boy or a dog-loving Hombre you're trying to lure into your space. Overtip him so that he likes the gig and wants to come around more often.

Masseur. Your doggy day spa should have an ample staff of qualified professionals. Many dogs love the attention and sensation of a deep-fur massage. Find out what specialties the masseur offers. Gaysians make fabulous massage therapists, and many are knowledgeable about herbal remedies, Bach flower therapy, and alternative medicine. Before you hoist your pooch onto the table, be sure you know the rates.

Handler. Your show dog will need a professional handler if you've got your eye on the top prizes at a conformation show. Shop around to find a handler who's light on his feet, easy on the eyes, and heavy on the wallet. Don't bargain shop for a handler. Hire the most expensive queen you can find. Offer to pay for his Armani suits and sandals. If your handler is fabulous and thinks your dog is, too, you'll be on your way to a cushy skybox overlooking the Westminster Group ring.

Therapist. The pressures of a high-powered canine life can wear on your pooch. Eight professionals and a demanding gay owner can send any pup to the couch. A canine therapist will be well worth the $350 per hour. Ideally, find a Guppy or a Two-Spirits who dabbles in the supernatural so that you don't need to hire a psychic, too.

Pool boy. While you're advertising for all of the above, *you* might as well have a little fun. Conduct an exhaustive search, hold multiple interviews, and do not compromise. Find out all his strengths and weaknesses. Be strict about dress code. Ask all of the pertinent questions: Does he like dogs around while he works? Does he charge hourly? Is skimming extra? Does he require an actual pool?

DOGGY DAY CARE

Unless you're a Lady of Leisure or a trust-fund baby or have a live-in house boy, your puppy is likely to be home alone while you're at work. Many communities in the suburbs and the cities have doggy day care facilities. The home of the original doggy day care was an Upper West Side apartment on West 86th Street in Manhattan called the Yuppy Puppy. Entrepreneur Joe Sporn conceived of the business so that his German Shepherd Valkyrie (a good Teutonic name!) wouldn't get bored, destructive, or operatically vocal. Since then, doggy day care centers have been sprouting up in cities and 'burbs alike, and they offer a valuable service to dog owners. Because most of the day cares are set up like nursery schools, where the dogs interact, your dog will have to pass a basic temperament evaluation, be in good health, and not be psychotic to be accepted as a client. Doggy day care is an excellent way to exercise and socialize your dog, and he'll make new friends, too. (With any luck, your dog will befriend dogs owned by cute single guys, gay or heteroflexible.) The dogs have playtimes, nap times, snack times, birthday parties, lessons, and lots more.

Before signing Brunnehilde up, take a complete tour of the center you're interested in. Consider whether the staff is courteous and knowledgeable, the facility clean and spacious, and the management both owner and dog friendly. Price is no object when you're leaving Baby Hilde for a whole day or even longer. In addition to boarding services for weekends, some facilities have pools, grooming services, outdoor runs, and agility equipment. Your dog will have so much fun that he won't even miss you during the day. A special feature of day care franchise Camp Bow Wow is its video monitoring system, which dog owners can access from their office (or home) computers. Michael Monks, a Camp Bow Wow proprietor and Australian Shepherd owner from Midland Park, New Jersey says:

> Our clients are *pulled* in the door by their dogs because the dogs have lots of fun. Safety is our top priority, which is why our camp counselors are trained in canine behavior, health, first aid, and CPR. We also provide overnight boarding, which means your dog may have more fun on your next vacation than you do. When you pick up your dog, he'll be as worn out as you are. A surprisingly large percentage of our clientele is gay, partly due to our gay-friendly atmosphere, from the camp counselors all the way up to the corporate headquarters.

THE OTHER END OF THE RAINBOW LEASH

Building a relationship with your four-legged partner is much like the beginning of any life-affecting romance, except that you don't have to worry about the stigma of sex on the first "real" date.

Beginning your puppy's education is like setting the parameters of a new relationship. One of you vies for the position of control. Even if you are a proud card-carrying bottom, your role in this new relationship must be top dog. You as the human owner must be in control, the one who decides where your partner sleeps, where he pees, and most important, when he is to come. A puppy who's out of control actually thinks he's in control; it's his owner who's out of control.

The second most important aspect in any relationship is establishing a bond based on trust, need, and respect. Although having a boyfriend who's too needy can be problematic or, at best, annoying at parties, it's acceptable and desirable to have a canine partner who needs you. You want your dog to believe that he depends upon you for everything in the world. Your puppy should regard you as his surrogate dam. The puppy looked to his mom for his food, safety, and well-being. He trusted that mom would be there for him, and your assuming her responsibilities transfers that bond of trust and reliance to you.

The bond you establish with the puppy must not be one sided. Even if you're mesmerized by your puppy's fuzzy cuteness, you cannot let your infatuation govern your relationship. As Aretha soulfully spells, R-E-S-P-E-C-T lays the groundwork for any functional relationship. You don't earn your puppy's respect by paying for dinner at Le Cirque or sending his parents a centerpiece for Pesach—puppies are impressionable, but they're not gay teenagers. You gain a puppy's respect through clarity, directness, and authority.

Canines as a single-minded race subscribe to the pack-leader philosophy. Someone has to be in charge, and your puppy wants you to wear the chaps in the family. Butch it up as best you can. Some boys feel empowered when they don their chaps; others feel fabulous; others, positively dykey. If the role of top dog makes you squeamish, camp it up! Think Bea Arthur if you can't pull off John Wayne. Your puppy won't appreciate your silver screen impersonations, but he will recognize the voice of authority.

PUPPY HOMESCHOOLING

Accustom the puppy to his collar from day one. As you might expect, the collar is a control device. It's no picnic trying to grab a squirmy, slick, superfast little gremlin; the collar helps a lot. Every time you praise your puppy, hold him by the collar and chant of his greatness.

Puppies, like the rest of us, loved to be loved. Every hour of every day for the puppy's first week, get down on your knees, clap your hands, call his name, and say, "Come over here and give Daddy some lovin'." (See, it *is* no different than the first week of every gay man's perfect romance!) When the puppy comes running with his wiggly bottom and smiling, "licky" face, grab him by the collar, kiss his head, and praise him.

That's week one of homeschooling.

Week two begins the most critical component of the relationship—the *come* command. (No matter what *Men's Health* or *Cosmopolitan* says, this command can be taught only to canines. Men never come on command; sometimes they don't even come home.) The basis of your puppy's entire curriculum depends on his flawlessly obeying the *come* command.

Trainers recommend a variety of methods to teach the *come to Daddy* command. You can attach the puppy's leash or, alternatively, a twelve-foot line to his collar. Either of these methods can work, but you'll find yourself reeling in a squealing ten-pound puppy more times than not. Puppies don't like to be dragged into compliance—they have to want to come to you.

Keep in mind that the puppy's aim when running free in the yard is "catch me if you can!" This game is not rewarding for the owner unless Leo DiCaprio is the one buckled into the leather collar. Perpetuating this game of chase with a puppy drains patience and burns calories.

Longtime trainer and behaviorist Paul Loeb, in his book *Smarter Than You Think,* describes his revolutionary method of teaching the recall (come). He proposes that you throw an article at the puppy as an extension of your domain. In other words, no matter how far that puppy runs from you, you can still nail him with a balled-up sweat sock. Alternatively, you can fling a soft leather loafer. The object has to have enough mass to travel through the air, so don't throw a pair of nylons, an emery board, or a boa. Be sure it's nothing that could hurt the puppy; don't throw a six-inch pump, which could knock a twelve-week-old puppy out, and don't fling your ruby glass slipper either (how will you get home?).

Loeb's contention is that the puppy, so impressed by your ability to throw, will instantly come running to you in amazement. Huh? Obviously Loeb's method is geared toward straight men and lesbians only. How many fags besides Billy Bean do you know who can throw?* If you're going to give this method a try, you'd better practice throwing a balled-up sock on your own before trying to impress your puppy. There's nothing worse than watching your puppy buckled over in laughter as you demonstrate your mother's pitching arm! Sporting dogs, especially retrievers, may never recover from the experience, and you may never regain their respect.

Kidding aside, a lucky throw can hit the puppy twenty feet away, and he may respond by coming to you, whose smell is all over that sock or slipper. Smelling you reminds him that you represent "home" and "security," thus your ruby slipper *actually* says, "There's no place like home."

Never underestimate your puppy's intelligence. Just as the dam trains her pups from the day their eyes open, so you begin working with the puppy on the day he arrives home. Despite their ability to throw and perform other primate activities, humans are inferior to dogs on many levels. All of the dog's senses—often including common sense—are superior to those of humans. Dogs instinctively know that they're members of a superior race, and it takes some doing to convince them otherwise. Think about the dog's senses. A Bloodhound or a Basset Hound can outsmell a human by 100,000 times. A Greyhound or a Whippet can outsee and outrun a human by miles, literally. A German Shepherd Dog or a Pharaoh Hound can outhear a human, picking up noises that are imperceptible to humans at every decibel.

Dress the Part

Your role as dominatrix, head school matron, and parliamentarian does not require any particular apparel. Best to begin your lessons wearing sensible shoes—a low heel, no flip-flops (even if they're Italian), and no slippery soles. You are likely to be running, chasing, and fetching. Avoid clothing that makes noise when you move, which includes beaded jackets, sequined head gear, and biker shorts. Your puppy's apparel—equally important—consists of a single accessory: a collar. The ideal collar to begin training is the martingale, consisting of a double loop that tightens as pressure is applied. Choke collars, pinch collars, and spike collars have no place in the classroom. Leave them in the bedroom.

**Footnote: The great American pastime is the straightest, dullest sport in the world. Billy Bean is the only living "out" switch hitter retired from the major leagues. Leave it to Glenn Burke, the first known gay MLB player, to invent the high five . . . who knew he was thinking "Fabulous!" as he reached home plate? Professional football boasts a few "out" punters and receivers: Dave Kopay, Roy Simmons, and Esera Tuaolo. Go long, ladies!*

Examples of the dog's superior common sense abound. Unlike gay men, dogs aren't manipulated by meaningless labels, superficial affairs, or models in Versace swimwear. Seems that dogs are naturally good character judges, know when they're being "handled," and think with their noses instead of their hyperboles. A favorite Leo Cullum cartoon in *The New Yorker* depicts a Poodle chatting with a Cocker; the caption says: "Jimmy Choo, Manolo Blahnik—honestly can't taste the difference." Does this sum up the dog's common sense, the Poodle's superior taste buds, or the folly of $1,000 pumps? Gay men will never know.

Not only can dogs be trained to maneuver complex obstacle courses at agility trials, but they also can be trained to detect bombs, narcotics, accelerants, human remains, cancer cells, and truffles. Dogs can be trained to hunt birds, herd sheep, protect property, rescue lost Swiss tourists, and not chew Jimmy Choo slingbacks (nothing worse than a pair of chewed Choos!).

Do not underestimate what your puppy can understand and comprehend. Young children can learn a foreign language in a few months. Puppies should be spoken to in English, not baby talk or robot talk. Granted, some Eurofags have instructed their au pairs to train their Papillons to sit, stay, and fetch in French, but not every dog is as bright as a bilingual Pap.

What's worse than conversing with your dog in French is translating your thoughts into D-O-G. Speak to your dog in complete sentences. Dogs recognize tone of voice and sounds and don't want their owners barking "sit/stay, sit/stay, stay, stay" at them for twenty minutes.

In other words, be yourself. Talk to your dog the way you talk to your friends. Sit your Bichon on his daybed and tell him, "Girlfriend, sit your powderpuff behind on that pillow until I get home from Splash," or "Stop stealing daddy's eighty-dollar designer sports briefs!" A key word in the English language, and most others, is *no*. Although the majority of trainers practice positive training techniques, the negative word remains unavoidable. Make every effort to be a *yes* man, but don't be afraid to reprimand the puppy for stealing your 2(x)ist thong or unweaving your welcome mat. Don't overuse "no," or the puppy will be as bored with "no/no/no" as he is with "sit/sit/sit." Remember: a bored puppy is a deaf puppy.

Another common misunderstanding about training puppies is that you must keep every lesson to two minutes or less. If a puppy can concentrate on unraveling your rug or flossing with your new 2(x)ist for fifteen or twenty minutes, what makes trainers believe that the young canine has a two-minute attention span? A puppy's attention span is at least equal to that of an average Pixie or Biscuit. Young gay men have notoriously short attention spans and, like puppies, are easily distracted by more interesting sights and smells. Puppies bore easily, too. What could be duller than "down/down/down" or "give-it-to-me/give-it-to-me" coming from a whiny old queen before dinner?

To keep puppies (and young boys) from becoming bored, you have to be direct and let them comprehend your intention. You have to convince these young charges that their very existence depends on your every word. Tell them that you're a casting agent for Abercrombie & Fitch . . . and that there's only one correct response to each command ("Down, boy").

Puppy training can be even more frustrating than dating trophy boys or chasing print models. Do not let the puppy convince you that he's too young, too flighty, or too cute to pay attention. Be the queen in command, and that puppy will be your loyal servant. Like actors and models, puppies are fond of role playing and will relish the opportunity to be the center of attention. They love when it's all about them.

To train your puppy, you must truly know your dog, including his liabilities and limitations. Your perfect puppy is a member of a flawed race, despite his thinking that he's superior to you and your human kind. Here's a short list of his shortcomings:

- dogs are stingy—they would rather rumble than share;
- dogs are related to coyotes and jackals—they would rather be wild and unruly than collared and tugged around;
- dogs are con artists—they lie, cheat, steal, and never confess;
- dogs live for bribes;
- dogs are catholic and Catholic—all accepting and very guilt ridden;
- dogs depend on the kindness of strangers and always take advantage of it;
- dogs think nothing of licking, biting, and humping grown men in public places (well, no one's perfect).

COMING OUT—THE SOCIAL LIFE

Once you've taught your puppy to come to you reliably both indoors and out, it's time to plan his cotillion. Your puppy is ready to "come out" to the world. Dogs by nature are social creatures. They would make ideal guests at a cocktail party: they love meeting new people and other dogs. They'll rub noses with virtual strangers, especially if they smell finger food or old money.

Proper canine socialization can mean the difference between a happy, easygoing, dog-friendly dog and a psychopathic, one-fag-only canine who hates, shuns, or is anxious around every dog and new person he meets. The latter pup might fit in at a party at Donatella's summer-house but not one hosted by Noel Coward. When introducing your puppy to the world, you must remain in control of the proceedings. You give your puppy the OK to meet and greet. The puppy regards you as his parent and party host. A parent doesn't let his child talk to strangers, so don't let baby Cher associate with every gypsy, tramp, and thief she meets in Central Park.

If the tramp from the park is a friend, or fairly recent trick, allow him to pet your puppy but don't allow him to whisk her out of her stroller and cuddle her. Spare your puppy the trick's insincere advances—been there, done that. Like the Old Testament God, you are a jealous deity and don't permit your servant to worship (or be worshipped by) lesser homosexuals. Your puppy waits for permission to greet the oncoming gypsy (aka Equity actor in Central Park) before the tails start wagging. Permitting just any Cher groupie to maul your puppy can confuse her, making her think she can bond and exchange puppy kisses with anyone. Not just any tramp can have his way with your pup. A young puppy is impressionable, and your bond is equally precious.

If by chance you are socializing your puppy on foot, that is, without a fabulous stroller, you've already started introducing him to his rainbow leash. You can't carry the puppy around forever. For most people, leash training occurs while the rest of the lessons and carols are going on. What's most important about leash training is how the puppy perceives the man on the other end of the rainbow. It's the top dog who's walking baby dog: you are the man in control. You are the one whom he looks up to for permission, guidance, and the occasional dried liver treat.

Meeting other dogs is just as important as meeting those acquaintances in the park. Parents don't want their human kids to pick up bad habits and lice from the dirty kids down the block, and puppy parents should be equally concerned. Making sure your puppy doesn't pick up behavioral and eight-legged tic(k)s requires caution. It's best not to let your puppy meet strange dogs until his inoculations are complete, but it's fine to let him scratch and sniff the familiar neighborhood dogs you know are vaccinated and healthy. So that your kid doesn't grow up socially retarded, don't wait until all of his shots are done to introduce him to the dogs you know. By six months of age, the puppy should be the most popular pup on the block, not the "daddy's boy" who's afraid of fleas and sleaze.

For the puppy's safety, a leash is attached on day one. No one instantly likes to be collared and tugged around; as you may know too well, this takes some getting used to. Once the puppy realizes he can't scratch his collar off, he resorts to trying to take control, running wild, pulling, tugging, and acting like his coyote cousins once removed.

If the owner has strongly bonded with his puppy, the puppy should stay near his all-knowing master; he shouldn't be lunging forward and barking at every passerby. Never let your dog drag you or pull you! Walking an out-of-control dog down the boulevard is not a pretty sight—it's hideous if you're in clogs or heels. Save the six-inch FM spikes for formal *heel* training—which I think is why they call it that.

Practice walking together in an enclosed area *without* a leash. See if you can get baby Toto to follow the yellow brick road with you skipping in front. (You don't need to be a big MGM Show Tune Queen to make this work, although a gingham jumper and basket add immeasurably to the proceedings.)

After a few days of yellow-brick-road work, it's time to try this with a leash. Once you attach the leash to Toto's collar, he'll automatically skip beside you. The leash is an extension of your control, but it's not your main device. Your little terrier should be obeying you and respecting your control before the leash is attached.

Toto, as we've discussed, was a very well-trained Cairn Terrier. Not an easy breed to train, especially with a horde of drunken dwarfs on the set. Even so, Toto was in more scenes than Judy, although he sang only half as well.

Manners and High Society

Smart, mannerly, and well groomed, Orlando, your Tibetan Terrier, sits patiently as the doorman unlocks the gate. Buxom and in full bloom, Orlando is welcome in every gay man's home, and the doors are held open.

If this Bel-Air scenario doesn't remind you of home, perhaps you're living in the wrong neighborhood or you have not placed proper emphasis on your dog's manners. For your dog to be welcome in your friends' homes and in chic public places, you must consciously undertake teaching him social "petiquette." Orlando's education goes beyond *sit* and *come*. He must walk politely on his leash, for you and his nanny; he must listen inside the home and out; he must accept the advances of (handsome) strangers and other dogs; and he must always smile at the paparazzi.

Visitors to your home should not have to politely ignore Orlando's gyrating upon their legs or nipping at their fingers. Not even gay men want to be around a rash and unruly Orlando, no matter how glassy blue his eyes or how bubblicious his movie star butt.

When your dog discourteously grabs your friend's Japanese Chin by the neck and throws him in the koi pond, you may never see your friend or his soggy Chin again. One simply doesn't dunk a Chin before teatime.

Structured learning time is key to teaching your dog good manners. Give Orlando props for good behavior, and soon he'll be acting like a civilized member of the Screen Actors Guild.

TOILETING, TOILETTES, AND TOIL

Did Barbie crate-train Beauty, her blonde Afghan Hound? After scrupulous research and no fewer than a dozen phone calls to the CEO of Mattel, the author has determined that yes, the blonde bimbo whom we grew up dressing in our closets indeed had the good sense to crate-train her Afghan puppy. Fortunately for Barbie and her high-heeled synthetic friends, Afghans are bright, clean dogs, although they can be stubborn at industry brunches and obedience trials. Had Barbie had to housebreak Snoopy, she might have had poopy pumps! Beagles aren't known for their tidy habits, and most aren't as bright as that famous high-flying, fast-typing trademark.

No matter which breed of puppy you own, the solution to house-training is politely enclosed in a wire crate. Because the attention span of most gay men for this topic is as unreliable as an infant puppy's bladder, let's quickly outline what you really need to know to keep your floors feces free and your drapes their original shade of eggshell.

- Feed your puppy twice a day, in the morning (before work, unless you're a Lady of Leisure or a retired Guppy) and in the early evening (right after tea dance or cocktails).
- Don't feed your puppy cheap food, even if you dine under the glow of the Golden Arches yourself. Select food with a good-quality protein source and a low filler and preservative content. Read the label. The better the food, the better the dog's nutrition, coat, and energy level, and the less the poop.

- Take the puppy outside ten to fifteen minutes after each meal. Let the puppy know that this is not a recreational outing: no balls, skipping, squirrel hunting, or boy chasing. This is a business trip.
- Choose a playroom for the puppy. Gate off a tiled or slate-floored room, or lift the rugs (no sense sacrificing an heirloom to piddle).
- Most puppies don't need an introduction to their crates. Just say "good, Beauty," and close the door. Give her a treat. If you've acquired a puppy from a good breeder, the puppy should already consider the crate her own room.
- Place the crate in the home wherever you are (the office, the living room, the bedroom). Just because the puppy is crated doesn't mean he

should feel isolated in his room. Think of the crate as the puppy's crib. How much time does an infant spend in his crib, snoozing, drooling, and staring at his rainbow mobile? Think of the puppy's gated quarters as his playpen. The puppy will spend unsupervised quiet time in his crate, including his daytime naps and nighttime sleep.

- Paper-training is to dog training what cloth diapers are to potty-training: antiquated, messy, and inconvenient. You'll abandon the idea the first time your intended paramour slides in the mud with his new Prada tennis shoes.
- City Girls and Guppies should take the puppy to the curb or sidewalk to do his business if no grassy patches are available. Pick up the pile, then pick up the puppy and go straight inside. Within a week, the puppy will piddle/poo the moment he feels the pavement.
- Do not put water in the crate. It spills out of the bowl and out of the puppy.
- Don't expect your puppy to remain in his crate for more than two or three hours, unless he's sleeping.
- If the puppy has an accident, clean it up and disinfect the area. Reasoning with the puppy over a twenty-minute-old turd won't impress the puppy. Watch more carefully next time.
- Some puppies are pee shy. Such a puppy usually waits for you to leave before he tinkles indoors because he's figured out that you have a thing about it. If he squats indoors in front of you, scream like the Merm on opening night. He won't stop (he can't), but he'll notice that you're wildly concerned and suddenly brassy. Pick him up and carry him outside while you finish your medley from *Gypsy* or *Happy Hunting*.

For queens who are partial to bell(e)s—carillons, chimes, southern boys—you might consider incorporating a potty bell into your house-training regimen. Hang a small bell on a string near the door that you and puppy use to go out for potty time. Each time you take him out to do his business, strike the bell with the puppy's paw. After a week or two of this routine, a bright puppy will ring the bell when he needs to go outside. If you have more than one dog, you can assign a different bell to each dog so you know which dog is pealing (or peeing). Show Tune Queens might be inspired to have eight dogs and train them to play "The Bells of St. Mary" or "Do-Re-Mi."

FIRST DAY OF SCHOOL

Homeschooling remains the first choice of doggy parents, gay and straight. Teaching a dog is really a 24/7 project, as the puppy is learning every minute of every day just by watching you, your partner, your friends, and the other dogs he meets. However, if you decide to take your puppy to an obedience class, you and your star pupil will have the advantage of some hands-on help from a professional trainer (who may or may not know something about dog behavior). Before signing up for an obedience class, ask the instructor's permission to audit a session to decide whether the class is for you. You want an instructor who's upbeat and positive, who doesn't use harsh methods, and who's comfortable with your lavender Poodle puppy.

In a class, you also have the advantage of learning from other owners and their ill-behaved mentees. Make sure that you bring the right collar and lead for your puppy (a martingale and a six-foot nylon lead) and that you dress smartly. If you're not the best dressed in the class, you're in grave danger. You'll disappoint the instructor and your fellow students. If you're not the best dressed homo in the class, then you're probably in Palm Springs and the whole class looks like a Calvin underwear audition. Keep your focus on the puppy, keep the class fun, and limit your cruising to after the lesson.

Obedience classes are best thought of as finishing school, a place where properly homeschooled young canine gents and ladies go to polish their manners. Try affecting a British or New England accent to give the puppy the idea that his *formal* training is underway. Prepare a basket of small sandwiches to offer as treats and share with the class. Perhaps pack a small carafe of plum wine for your favorite Calvin puppy dad.

A word about trainers: It's fine for you to hire a humpy gym bunny to spot you on the bench press on your weekly visit to the gym; it will give you the inspiration to put on your gym shorts and get there. Your puppy, believe it or not, doesn't need that kind of inspiration—you are the only man your puppy needs, no matter how inexperienced, flabby, or messy you look in your Daisy Dukes. The person your dog must learn to obey is you. It doesn't help you to have a puppy who obeys Joe Trainer instead of you. Even if some buff dog trainer promises to teach baby Esther advanced heelwork and synchronized swimming, save the money and resist the temptation—no matter what a great pool-party trick that would be (and cheaper than a pair of cabana boys)!

No Double Teaming

Your puppy can have only one top dog, so you and your partner cannot use the puppy's lessons as quality family time. Only one man on the puppy at a time. After the lesson is over, your partner can come and play with the puppy. Puppies like attention but prefer fun and games to listening and obeying. The puppy will beeline to your partner the minute he sees him, just to escape his "sit/stay" refresher course. Don't give the puppy his way, and don't let him be distracted by third parties when you're trying to teach him new lessons.

STUDS AND BITCHES: THE SECRET SEX LIVES OF DOGS

How could a gay book about dogs not discuss S-E-X? As remarkable as the canine tribe is, as versatile, talented, and athletic as dogs are, their sex lives are sadly very dull.

Not just because most of their sexual activity is heterosexual but also because there's surprisingly little action in the dog set. Male dogs, not unlike every other male, are ready, willing, and able 24/7; it's the females who ruin the party. Shocking.

Bitches, perhaps named for their twice-annual heat cycles, are open to sexual intercourse for only about 5 days twice a year. That leaves most poor hounds with 355 days a year to find action elsewhere. Monogamy, fortunately, isn't a virtue in the dog world. (Gay men aren't that well versed in it either.) Because humans largely govern the sex lives of dogs, there are some really lucky dogs, known as stud dogs and champion sires, and then there's a large horny pack of wild and crazy dogs that aren't getting "put on" anyone. Some top sires get to do their thing with as many as ten or more bitches a year; others may get lucky two or three times in their lives. Have you ever wondered why a show dog looks so damn happy when he wins Best in Show? It's not because he cares about the trophy, the title, or even his handler's happiness. No, a Best in Show win ensures he's getting laid a lot more often in the coming months. Did you see Rufus, the Colored Bull Terrier, jumping around the ring after he won Best in Show at Westminster in 2006? Is there any doubt what Romeo Rufus was thinking? Bull Terrier bitch booty!

IS MY DOG GAY, TOO?

Now, the inevitable question: Can dogs be gay? We know for sure that dogs are regular attendants of the country's pride parades, but does that qualify them as gay? We know that there are some breeds in which the male dogs tend to be a bit more queer than in other breeds. One French Bulldog breeder says, "You can keep two Frenchie boys together: they're like a couple of old gays, but the girls fight all the time." But are these Frenchies really gay? We also know that the gay influence on certain breeds has added fabulousness to these breeds. Do you think the Bichon Frisé would look like that in the ring without queer pioneers leading the way? How gay is a show Maltese, Afghan Hound, or Standard Poodle?!

The real question is: Can dogs be homosexual? After many years of spying on dogs in their most private moments, I am convinced that all male dogs are bisexual. The same might be said for human beings, too, had religion, society, and Republicans not interfered. Dogs don't believe in Jesus or send money to Pat Robertson, they don't look down at lesbians for adopting children or teaching public school, and they don't vote. (If they did, they definitely wouldn't have voted for "W.") Thus, dogs have no inhibitions about whom they sniff, lick, or hump. Male dogs don't have to worry about being excommunicated, fired, or deprived of basic rights if they're caught getting a little frisky with the neighbor's cute boy Bichon in the lavender bow.

Given the lack of available female attention and the virtual outlawing of canine concubines in nicer neighborhoods, most male dogs in suburbia are horny creatures. Dogs not only don't care whether they hook up with male or female dogs but also aren't even that picky about the species. Male dogs will happily hump humans' legs (and furniture legs and couches, too). Yes, they are really trying to get off: it's instinctive and good old naughty doggy-style fun, until someone flings them off. Every self-respecting male has got to give it a try!

If you own a female dog and she's humping your leg or another dog, probably a male, she is indeed a dominatrix. Don't panic—buy her a whip and let her enjoy her role as top bitch. In the dog world, the female is usually the dominant pack member, and she calls the shots. (She's got the neatest box in the woods and she knows it.)

In most species, females aren't as keen to rock 'n' roll as the males are. Even in the wild, not every female wolf gets to have a litter; only the alpha bitch is permitted to breed, and the other females act as maiden aunts and nannies. This social structure is designed to preserve the species so that only the best animals breed and the pack concentrates on raising, feeding, and protecting one litter of pups at a time.

In the purebred dog world, breeders determine which dogs get to breed by holding dog shows. If you thought the wolves in the woods had it bad, consider their cousins in the world of dog showing—a true dog-eat-dog contest. Dog shows are intended to be the testing ground of breeding stock, although they rarely achieve this end. Sadly, like everything else today, dog shows are more about politics, money, advertising, sexual favors, and egos than about the dogs and their breed standards. Quite a few judges know surprisingly little about canine anatomy and structure, think they know more than the breeders who specialize in their breeds, and spend more time picking their outfits for the group rings than they do studying breed standards. And these aren't only the gay judges!

Not every dog breeder cares about winning in the show ring, although most do. It's a real test of will to finish (earn a championship on) a good dog in the more popular breeds, especially in rings in which there are leagues of professional handlers. Too often judges pick handlers and not dogs—some handlers can make a mediocre dog shine brighter than a great dog handled by a mediocre or average handler.

Given their druthers, show dogs prefer to be in the winner's circle, whether it be with an overpaid professional handler or with a really talented owner-handler. Bringing home the ribbons means more than chopped sirloin for dinner—it can mean a year-long booty tour. He's king for a year! So as not to deflate His Majesty's confidence, the girl-dog subjects come to him, the smelliest bitches being shipped directly to the stud's royal chambers.

A stud's got to perform on cue every time. There are no fluffers on this set! Daddy's making good money for every successful *tie*—a term that deserves a definition. (Who can expect you to know the ins and outs of hetero canine sex when you still wince at the words *bosom* and *vulva*?) The tie is made after the penis is successfully inserted into the vagina; a bulbous swelling at the base of the penis prevents retraction until after ejaculation. That's why you can't separate a copulating pair of canines with a garden hose or naked photographs of Star Jones Reynolds. Hetero sex is just plain scary!

PROMISCUITY AND THE BIG FIX

For once gays have no bone to pick with the Vatican. Promiscuity and premarital sex are indeed sinful and ruinous . . . for our dogs. Holy hypocrites, Batgirl! Gay men do not want little Colin spilling his seed all over town any more than we want little Buffy to spawn vampire Pugabulls. You cannot teach your dog to practice abstinence or safe sex—not even the Italian or Irish ones. There's nothing moral or immoral about canine sex. Your Boston Terrier, a good Catholic breed, doesn't have to be emotionally ready for his first boff, bonk, or bang. Dogs and cats don't have souls and don't need "saving," even though my mother is still praying for her white Angora "Prudence," whom she is firmly convinced is in Purgatory for being a

screeching whore. Thankfully, the Church does not care whom your Colin humps or to whom Buffy gives away her booty. There's only one way to fix a potentially broken heart or hymen.

If you're trying to get a group of guys to spill cosmos in unison, just say, "Castration!" Few topics are as unpopular with gay men. In fact, straight men are equally protective of their 'nads and those of their canine pals. It's a guy thing. We don't like the idea of our dogs being transformed into castrati or eunuchs in front of our eyes. There are already enough trannies to go around. We have less problem with ovario-hysterectomy because that just sounds like a surgical procedure, and we can't readily envision it.

Now let's talk briefly about spaying and neutering dogs. Spaying, technically ovariohysterectomy, is a surgical procedure that removes the female's sex organs. Neutering is the surgical removal of the male's testicles. There are towers of research on spaying/neutering, and no one agrees on anything except that spaying/neutering reduces the number of unwanted dogs in shelters and city pounds. The vast majority of breeders and veterinarians recommend spaying/neutering pet dogs to prevent potential cancers in both sexes. Some breeds are more prone to cancer than others, but it's peace of mind knowing that the likelihood of testicular, breast, and ovarian cancers are minimized if not eliminated.

The question of when to spay or to neuter a pet remains a controversial matter. Some veterinary studies recommend spaying/neutering when the animals are as young as six weeks of age, although such a radical approach best applies to puppies born in shelters. It's better to adopt out sterilized puppies than to put them in the hands of good-intentioned owners who neglect to have them spayed or neutered at the proper age. Most breeders recommend not having the dog neutered or spayed until he or she is six months of age. Certain breeds that mature slowly shouldn't be altered until they are at least one year of age, especially the males. Breeds with large heads and deep chests, such as some of the Sporting and Working breeds, don't develop properly without hormones in their systems until they are one or even two years of age. Your breeder is the best person to advise you when is the opportune time to have the dog fixed.

Modern veterinary scientists are currently developing immunocontraceptive vaccines, which are administered by injection and could make spaying and neutering surgeries a thing of the past. Gay men will surely rest easier knowing that little Lukas doesn't have to lose his golden globes. Actually, these days your veterinarian can even replace your male dog's testicles with implants so that the dog doesn't miss them. Although gay men would *never* be vain enough to invest in cosmetic surgery for themselves, it's worth it so that your little guy doesn't feel self-conscious in the dog park. Keep in mind that you cannot show an altered dog in an AKC dog show, although the UKC does offer conformation classes for spayed and neutered dogs. In both clubs, altered dogs can compete in performance trials such as obedience and agility trials.

Hooking Up at the Dog Run

An afternoon romp in the Chelsea dog run may yield a few promising cell-phone numbers for you, but the chances of your well-dressed city dog's finding action in the park are limited. Unhooked dogs of every shape and size litter the dog run, and not a one is hooking up. A feisty bitch gushing with attitude is bound to catch the eye and nose of your poor horn dog, Cooper. As pervasive as the sights and smells of saucy bitches in the air may be, every one of those delish swishers has an officious mommy figure guarding her fanny. Even in Lower Manhattan, poor Cooper just can't get a break. Sex in the park used to be one of the small pleasures of city life we took for granted. Now the park is just a G-rated fashion parade!

SEXUAL PROBLEMS

Sexual problems are a nuisance in every species, although dogs rarely have to deal with erectile dysfunction or the infelicitous pairing of two tops. Yet the males of both species tend to exhibit their virility in demonstrative ways, namely mounting and humping every vertical object in their paths and sponsoring parades to legalize this behavior in public. Dog pride parades tend to be held in obscure villages and get very poor media attention, another sign of apparent discrimination. Gay parades tend to get better coverage, especially from the liberal newspapers and a certain closet queen from *The New Republic.*

Mounting is an activity that should be discouraged from the onset, as should a male dog's marking indoors on furniture, drapes, and even your leg. Such behavior can be a nuisance, particularly when he hasn't asked your permission or offered to buy you a drink first. There's a certain machismo about leg lifting, but peeing on the master is an unattainable privilege in most households.

A guy always feels proud the first time he sees his young boy pup lifting his leg on a fence or the living room ficus tree. For male dogs, marking behavior is a territorial activity as opposed to a sexual one. Correct the dog on the spot, and disinfect the area. You might be wise to wear leather pants until the behavior is extinguished completely. Altered dogs tend to mark less than unaltered dogs do, although both will continue to hump with or without the equipment to activate.

Female sexual problems include pseudo-pregnancy, in which an unbred, unaltered bitch imagines that she's pregnant. She will nest and even adopt a doll as her baby. Gay men should hide their Ken dolls and offer the dog gherkins and low-fat vanilla-bean Häagen-Dazs. It's senseless to argue with a clingy hormonal bitch who's flipped her wig. Her phase will pass in a few days.

Anal Sacs Fifth Avenue

Fear not, 'possums: we're going to talk about shopping, not about those smelly, irritable little scent glands known as anal sacs. If you ever see your power pup dragging his derriere along the pavement on Fifth Avenue, he is not cuing you to stop at Bloomingdales. He's a little impacted.

The anal sacs, which contain glands, are found on either side of the dog's anal vent, just beneath the skin, opening to the outside by tiny ducts. Normally, the sacs remain empty, as they are squeezed and drained during bowel movements. If your dog is constantly licking at his anus, he is not showing off—he is uncomfortable and may need to have his glands expressed.

No gay man expresses his own dog's anal sacs. The violently rotten smell of the fluid that's secreted (and the potential to stain your suede pants) is unfathomable. Take Pepé to the vet, and step out of the room. It's clear this is no laughing matter, as impacted anal sacs can mean that the dog is suffering from a bacterial infection or even an abscess.

Now that we've gotten that out of the way, let's haul ass down to Bergdorf's and see if they've marked down that lizard skin pea coat!

SACS

SHARING YOUR LIFE

For homebodies and their spoiled pets, a dog's life can be great fun. Your dog will love quality time with his favorite person, especially on rainy Saturdays when you're stranded together or on any other lazy afternoons.

Aside from just "hanging out" time, set aside some structured time each week for your dog, maybe ten minutes in the evening before supper or before bedtime. Don't just practice obedience commands—that's as dull as rereading college textbooks. Apply the commands to indoor doggy games. Have the dog sit/stay while you hide freshly baked treats around the house. Nothing's as exciting as finding a fresh bone under your pillow! You can also devise games with miniature marshmallows, oyster crackers, tennis balls, and anything else that's lo-cal or fun to chase.

For domestic divas and other meticulous Homemakers, baking is an art that won't be wasted on your connoisseur canine. Incorporating healthy dog ingredients into easy recipes can be the perfect "inning" for your four-legged kids. Every time your pastry-pup sees you get out your apron and rolling pin, he'll be dancing for joy. And who doesn't like to lick the bowl? You won't have to worry about the oven timer because your dog will never let you forget what's in the oven as the aroma of bacon, cheese, and rising dough wafts through the house. Julia would be so pleased.

PARTY PLANNING

Of course, Homemakers can cook, too! Prepare a special doggy meal for your dog's birthday, Halloween, or another special occasion. If your dog's the love of your life, why not Valentine's Day? Just keep that between us. Your friends and your boyfriend will not understand and may stage an intervention.

If you have friends who "get it," then consider hosting a dog party. A dog party is an authentic theme party, which of course gay men invented during the Renaissance. A discarded chapter from *The Da Vinci Code* reveals how Leonardo and Michelangelo cohosted the first gay theme party (a White Party, of course, attended by hot Italian boys and other scantily clad cherubs). And there's much documentation about those gay society Drag Balls during the other renaissance in Harlem. Thus history teaches us that only gay men can throw truly fabulous theme parties.

Although most gay men don't need a reason to party, you'll need to make up something for the invitation. Yentas, of course, can plan a bark mitzvah for their puppolas. Obedience school graduation, a finished Canine Good Citizen or championship title, and the puppy's first birthday are all great reasons to throw a party. Any one of these parties could be hosted at your dog's day spa, but sometimes it's fun to be the hostess with the mostest of your own puppy ball.

When planning a dog party, it's important to get a nice mix of well-behaved pooches and their sociable owners. Be careful to invite only friends whose dogs are well socialized and reliable around other dogs. Never invite dull people to parties, even if you're related to them. And avoid anyone who has a pain-in-the-ass dog, unless his owner is single, cute, and under thirty. There's nothing worse than a rowdy retriever stealing all the treats and humping the host's MinPin!

Table manners are key, especially if you decide to host a formal tea for your friends with civilized canines. Etiquette is alive and well in the gayborhood. Frenchies and Pugs, for example, love any event that involves crumpets and clotted cream—who doesn't?—and few guests look as lovely in a badger collar and pillbox hat.

Bling Party Dolls

Host a doggy bling party! If housewives can sell costume jewelry, kitchen gadgets, and streaky makeup at home parties, dog-loving gays can peddle doggy bling! Your corner doggy boutique likely would love to present the latest in canine couture to a group of your dog-owning friends and their well-behaved pocket pups. Doggy bling caters to the small and fancy dogs, so don't invite Size Queens with their slobbery Great Danes or gym bunnies with their Goldens or Pointers.

A garden brunch is always a hit with gay men. Naturally, civilized dogs are partial to a well-planned brunch menu. Assign each owner a treat to prepare for the dogs: mini liver quiches, bacon-bit scones, tunamisu, lamb and rice salad, and wheat and barley muffins are just a few savory examples that the author has perfected at bruncheons. Check out Cheryl Gianfrancesco's yummy book *Doggy Desserts: Homemade Treats for Happy, Healthy Dogs* for some expert guidance. For attendees who don't bake, be sure to give them the address of a good doggy bakery in town. There are always online "barkeries," such as the HoundsTooth Bakery (www.houndstoothbakery.com). The host should make sure that there's human food available as well as a case of bubbly. The invitation to drink before noon makes any party irresistible. Hell, the Bloody Mary was named after a vicious fag at brunch! If your friends can't cook, bake, or mix cocktails, find some *gay* friends or hire a caterer and a humpy bartender.

Speaking of staff for your dog party, you might also want to hire some entertainment, especially if the bartender refuses to dance on a box. Consider a doggy fortune teller to read the dogs' paws and tell horoscopes. Another popular option is a doggy masseur, but these professionals can be costly, especially the ones who refuse to use flavored oils or strip on the box.

Use your creativity and make up some party games for the dogs, which should revolve around the treats and the dogs. Games of fetch, Frisbee, doggy races, and follow the lesbian are perennial favorites. If the party gets a little slow, there's always bobbing for hotdogs!

Drag Queen Safety Tips

Inevitably a Drag Queen will find her way to your dog party. Like Bloodhounds, Drag Queens can smell a single drop of Ketel One within a ten-mile radius. It's important to discuss dress code for dog parties, especially when fancy gays and cross-dressing divas are attending. Generally wide-brimmed sun hats and lace gloves are appreciated for an outdoor get-together on a sunny day, but keep in mind that young puppies are impressionable and easily frightened. Discourage the cavalier use of parasols and any hats that could have been featured in the finale of a Howard Crabtree musical. Dogs with instinctive gaydar—the top gay breeds—will recognize a frightful ensemble and possibly be scarred for life. Drag Queens should also be kindly asked to wear flats so that their size fourteen heels don't inadvertently flatten a Pekingese puppy into a toaster treat. A Pup-Tart, as it were.

MOVIE NIGHT

Plan a Jiffy Pop night with your dog. He will love hanging out on the sofa with you for movie night, whether it's an all-camp night or an action movie night. Most dogs love the voice of Bette Davis. *All About Eve* is a delicious choice. All

THE SMITHS
DEPECHE
MODE
Soft
Cell

seven seasons of *Buffy*—a perfect vacation week at home! Movie musicals also make dogs' tails wag. If show tunes aren't your thing, a Matt Damon marathon cannot disappoint. Dogs love hearing barking on TV, so consider movies with starry mutts such as Benji, Lassie, or Liza Minnelli. As long as there's popcorn (unsalted) and lots of petting, however, dogs don't care who's starring in the flicks: it can be any gay fave such as Brad Pitt, Lukas Ridgeston . . . or both! (Whose tail's wagging now?)

Dressing Them Up!

For arts and craft wonks who can knit or sew, you can have great fun designing and making costumes for your hip pooches. Dressing up dogs may seem frivolous and even pointless, but it doesn't have to be. On your next trip to Gun Barrel City, Texas, or Mobile, Alabama, think how many hot Texans and 'Bama boys may raise their barrels when they meet your Staffy dressed up in his chaps and leather vest. Next time you're shaking it in Salt Lake City, bring your Frenchies all dolled up like Donny and Marie, and see what a warm welcome you get from the Mormon folk. The boys in Back Bay will worship your Boston Terrier looking immaculate in his Cenacle of the Holy Gucci school uniform. Visit any of the red states during the next campaign season and see how much the folk enjoy seeing your MinPin high stepping down the avenue in his Boy Scout uniform. Why not give them ideas for another ill-fated Constitutional amendment! Speaking of right-wingnuts, visit Dorothy's home state of Kansas with your Cairn Terrier dressed up as Laura Bush—stop by the Phelps home in Topeka and leave a memento on the doorstep.

KNITTING

Straight readers thumbing through this book will think "knitting" is gay lingo for something that our grandmothers didn't do . . . and they'd be wrong. Yes, men knit, and some of them are gay, too. The history of men knitting is a fascinating and romantic one, tracing back to artsy Vikings in the ninth century, creating tasteful Norwegian sweaters and darning nets on bitching big barges. Knitting, sewing, and crocheting, gay men have a penchant for creating clothing. Perry Ellis was born with a silver thimble in his mouth. Gay men who knit can use their handy talents to keep their dogs warm and stylish. There's more than one book on the topic, including volumes on doggy patterns, instructions, and illustrations. Our favorite is *Men Who Knit and the Dogs Who Love Them.* It's a keeper.

GETTING OUT

Most dogs, even the laziest lapdog and the densest Bulldog, love to get outside and enjoy the fresh air. Throwing a ball for the dog to retrieve or flinging a Frisbee is the easiest to do in your own backyard. Your canine pal will love the time spent together, and he'll look forward

A TRIP TO DR. FEELGOOD

When powder and mascara won't cheer up your glum Pekingese, whom you regrettably and coincidentally named Joan Livers, you may have to consider a special kind of outing to meet the lady with "the knife." Although lesbians in WeHo succeeded in banning the declawing of cats a few years ago, there are no laws (yet!) about surgically improving our canine girlfriends. Why should Scones be the only ones to enjoy the lift of a new belly or a perky face? Although the Europeans consider us American barbarians for docking and cropping our dogs—those high-minded Continental types don't even dock their boys—cosmetic surgery on many breeds of dogs is as commonplace as BOTOX in California.

Among the cosmetic procedures available for our sagging canine pals are skin-fold removal, tummy tucks, breast reductions, dental enhancement, and testicular implants. A facelift on a Basset Hound or Shar-Pei will not add nobility to your dog, but it can decrease rashes and unsightly lines. Tummy tucks and liposuction can hide the rolls on a Bulldog, especially after she's had a litter or two. It's not easy regaining your girlish figure after delivering ten or eleven kids!

Cosmetic dentistry, geared toward straightening, repairing, and replacing crooked, tilted, broken, or missing teeth, offers dogs many real benefits. A dog's whole world is in his mouth, or so he believes. If your dog's bite is crooked, you can even investigate canine orthodontics, and put Vanity in braces to keep her smiling straight at you. Keep your dog's teeth white by brushing them frequently, although embarrassing discoloration can be brightened and whitened at the vet's office.

Testicles are another matter—a matter of manly honor and ego. Testicular implants, made of silicone or plastic, for neutered dogs restores the dog's (and the owner's) swagger and self-assurance. Gregg Miller invented and patented these implants in 1997, and gay men are always willing to salute any guy who has his eye on the ball.

By the way, show dogs must rely on their natural, unretouched beauty and cannot be surgically enhanced or manipulated . . . until they're retired. The author would never encourage a show-dog owner to improve his otherwise perfect dog by taking him to a local cosmetic surgeon. You're much wiser to do what Peter Allen did—go to Rio! The Brazilian doctors are fabulous, and so are the boys at Sorelle Margherita!

to these daily sessions with you even if they're only ten or twenty minutes. For dogs that love to get their feet wet, the ones that aim for every puddle on a walk, consider purchasing a kiddie wadding pool. Your aquatic pal will get hours of fun, splashing and jumping. You can even encourage small dogs to retrieve a toy or a treat.

If you work out at the gym, save some of your cardio time to spend with your dog. If you're unable to find a gym or there isn't one in a fifty-mile radius (?!), you can spend a little time outdoors exercising your dog. If running or jogging is in your regimen, your dog may be a willing and able partner (assuming you've selected a breed that's able to keep up with you for the duration of your run). Even a small dog can run around a couple of blocks and will revel in the chance to keep up with you. If you have a Sporting breed, you can even train the dog to run next to your bicycle. Keep in mind the dog's safety and your own when undertaking a cycling tour of the neighborhood. Untangling a Bichon from the spokes of your Huffy will be distressing, to say the least.

In the right ensemble, Rollerblading with your Golden Retriever or Airedale smacks lusciously of Queer Fit America. Glide at a safe, steady speed. If you're going too fast, your best features blur, and there's little point cruising at sixty miles per hour.

Adventurous guys can include their dogs on a hiking or backpacking excursion. How butch is this?! If not, you probably have a backpack somewhere in the house that bears the name of a fragrance designer. You can always borrow a backpack from the lesbian next door or your brother-in-law or go to the local sporting goods store to buy one (any excuse to check out the new clerks at Dicks or the Sports Authority!). For the fashion conscious, consider a backpack by Puchibag, which comes in an array of colors from khaki to pink. Your Toy dog will cozily stow away for your outing. You can purchase a backpack for your larger dog online or at a

Sunday in the Park

Take your Labrador Georgette to the local dog park for some off-leash freedom. If you're lucky, you'll even have a privately run dog park to explore. The private dog parks tend to be cleaner, safer, and supervised. Yes, a park can be all those things and still be fun—it's a dog park, not a sex club. Not every community has a dog park, public or private, but you can search online for one near your home. If you're lucky enough to be gay in one of the dog-park hubs, you (and your pooch) will have lots of options for cruising and untethered merriment. Among the best cities to live with your dog are New York City, San Francisco, Portland, Seattle, and Atlanta. Following the lead of Pug Hill in New York's Central Park, recently a band of gay college boys and local Twinks founded Dachshund's Creek.

pet-supply store, but don't expect the dog to carry *all* your shit. Hiking along a trail in a state or local park won't require a large backpack—you're not going across Central Europe. Be sure to pack water and a bowl, the dog's leash and collar, a first-aid kit, bug spray, and your cell phone (to call your lover to pick you both up once you're lost or tired).

GARDENING

If your backyard isn't getting much action these days, perhaps it's time to channel your Inner Martha Stewart. Gardening is where it's at! Not just terriers and the feds are good at digging; just about any dirty dog loves to get his paws muddy. Although it's fun to involve your dog in your weekend activities, you don't want your Norfolk Terrier practicing his excavation techniques on your heirloom dahlia bulbs. Once your dog sees you taking a spade to your edible-flower bed, he'll take that as an invitation to your garden party and dig in with two feet.

If the dog really loves to dig, you can designate an out-of-the-way area that is his personal garden (perhaps in your neighbor's yard!) or build a sandbox (with a cover to keep the neighbor's cat from leaving souvenirs). In fact, lots of dogs don't like to get their feet wet or dirty.

You can train your dog to participate in yard work, depending on what size dog you have. Medium-size dogs can carry garden tools, while large dogs, equipped with harnesses, can learn to pull a wheelbarrow or a cart.

Enjoying your dog outdoors in the fresh air and sunshine should be a rewarding time for both man and dog. Next to the safety of your prize-winning peonies, your dog's well-being in the garden should spring to mind. Keep sharp garden tools and potentially lethal fertilizers away from the dog. Some mulches use cocoa hulls, which can be toxic to dogs as well.

SHOPPING

With your pooch smartly stowed away in an alligator tote or heeling well on a sequined lead, the two of you can share one of gaydom's most beloved indoor sports: shopping! Most chic boutiques and exclusive department stores will happily hold the door open for you and your furry special friend. Although owners encounter vile non-dog-friendly individuals in our civilized society, Fifth Avenue retailers recognize a valuable customer (and a Louis Vuitton pet carrier). You'd be surprised how chatty and accommodating the stock boys become when you've got a Japanese Chin in tow. Even retailers on Worth Avenue, Palm Beach, will let in a quality fag with a quality bag.

Now for our fave outdoor sport: at open-air markets and other outdoor trading posts vendors always welcome dogs, even if you're not in an upscale, gay-friendly community. Dogs would rather shop outdoors anyway, unless it's raining.

Woof!

AL FRESCO DINING

In some towns and cities, you can find outdoor cafés that cater to dog owners. Usually these eating establishments aren't too far from the dog park. Look into taking your dog out for a nice casual dinner. If he's well trained and will sit quietly under or near the table, you'll have a pleasant evening out together. Of course, in Europe, you can bring your dog to dinner every night, although it's costly to jet to Paris for escargot and the privilege. Some gay-friendly/dog-friendly states, such as California and Florida, allow dogs to dine with their owners outdoors—another good reason to visit Laguna Beach and Key West.

If Duval Street or the Champs Élysées aren't in your travel budget this week, you can always take your pup on a picnic in the park. A little Veuve Clicquot and snail salad will make you both forget about Gay Paree!

ANTIQUING AND ART COLLECTING

Many gay men have a passion for collecting things, and their dog breeds of choice often fuel their longing to unearth unimaginable treasures. Dogs have been the subject of *objets d'art* since the Pharaoh and his hounds posed for their family vases. Artisans from the Victorian period as well as the art nouveau and art deco periods have bequeathed gay men with good credit a plethora of irresistible things. Ebay becomes Egay when searching for over-the-top collectibles dedicated to your favored breed. For instance, popular Victorian-age breeds such as the Bulldog, the Frenchie, the Boston Terrier, and the Pug are immortalized on objects such as cigarette cases, salt and pepper shakers, automobile hood ornaments, teapots, decanters, napkin rings, and peppermills, not to mention inkwells, cigarette lighters, bookends, clocks, children's toys, ceramic and glass lamps, walking sticks, and humidors. Terrier fans will find that their feisty companions have inspired artisans for generations as well. Propelled by the love for your breed, you'll finally have something more to do at the fleece markets than basket shopping!

Of all breeds, Frenchies are the most celebrated in the collectibles field, largely due to the breed's popularity through the three movements, Victorian, art nouveau, and art deco. According to avid Frenchie collector Gary Bachman: "The Victorian depictions tend to be highly ornamented, while the art nouveau ones are elegant and sinuous. The art deco movement of the 1930s was a response to the Industrial Revolution and it provides us with pieces that are stylized and decorated in brilliant colors."

Similarly, the Pug enjoyed popularity through these important art movements. Pug breeders Bill Gorodner and Lloyd Alton observe: "Gay guys and decor are practically synonyms, and your Pug obsession can be expressed in many collectibles that look like your flat-faced, curly-tailed best friend. Because of the people of note who adore Pugs, the hobby of collecting Pug art, whether paintings, porcelain, or statuary, is practically unlimited and adds to the hauteur to which so many gay guys aspire."

In upscale communities, dogs are permitted to shop in tandem with their owners, especially if their owners are known customers of the emporium. It's imperative that your dog is well behaved, as there's nothing worse than a Bulldog in a china shoppe.

For real art enthusiasts, your dog can help you track down bronze sculptures and oil paintings until your bank account screams, "Uncle!" Art dealer William Secord of the Secord Gallery in Manhattan shares the following: "Gay men simply want the best they can find. In my gallery in New York City, some of our most loyal clients are gay men, and they avidly seek turn-of-the-century oil paintings of Cavaliers, Frenchies, Dandies, and Skyes." If the subject is *dogs in oil,* William Secord reigns as *the* world expert. Not only does Bill have a fabulous gallery on East 76th Street, specializing in nineteenth- and twentieth-century dog painting, he also has written a few hefty full-color encyclopedias on the subject. If you're in NYC, visit the gallery—Bill is a gracious, knowledgeable host, and he's got the classiest "Back Room" on the whole island!

If your AmEx or bank account won't handle a Maud Earl oil painting or a Fabergé French Bulldog sculpture, consider the fascinating and colorful world of antique doggy postcards. Ranging from movie stars and their dogs to fashionable ladies in period dresses, doggy postcards feature many classic breeds and come in a wide range of styles from Europe and America. Start your collection by visiting Paul Keevil's Web site (www.canineartconnections.com), which also features prints, posters, and much more. You'll be hooked in no time. You can also find vendors selling postcards at most dog shows and antique fairs.

The Gayborhood Dog Club

Why not start a gang? Organize a weekly get-together with the neighborhood dogs to go to the dog park, playground, local park, or outdoor shopping center. These social outings can brighten up an ordinary weekend and provide social time for both dogs and owners. Consider giving your dog club a name like the Chelsea Chompers or the Piedmont Pooches. Do a trademark search to make sure you're not stepping on some other queen's paws.

If you loiter in chat rooms a lot, you might consider getting your dog-owning buddy list to plan a weekend hookup. There are no laws against using your dog as bait for potential Internet romances. Remember, dogs love to be used, especially if it means meeting other dogs and their handsome owners. The most sophisticated of the cyber-homos, the Bears already have weekend pack parties, and lots of Bears have furry dogs at home in their caves.

THE RAINBOW TOUR: STEPPING OUT IN GAY SOCIETY

You don't have to be Madonna or Elton John to be on tour! You and your fabulous, well-trained pooch can hit the yellow brick road and begin chasing rainbows, ribbons, and trophies.

Explore the whole gamut of gay activities that attract dog owners and their dogs to the glamorous life. From dog shows and dance competitions to fashion shows, circuit parties, and over-the-top pride parades, every venue offers rewards and yummy trophies, though some are just shiny cups. Whether it's Mardi Gras in Sydney, the San Francisco Gay Pride Parade, or the *magnifique* Paris Dog Show, it's easy to get swept away in this world of Gays Gone Wild.

So many photo ops: pack your jewelry, thong, and product . . . there's a dog show in town! Competitive sports, fashion exhibitions, political rallies, charity balls, and vacations to dog-friendly gay resorts and beaches—the possibilities are limited only by your imagination, budget, and sense of adventure. For this grueling last chapter, permit your author to be your Julie McCoy and give you a deluxe tour of the big gay dog-loving world.

LE CANINE EXHIBITION

Dog showing is the gayest sport of all! Ooh la la! Although dog racing used to be called the "Sport of Queens," today the queens aren't at the track; they're primping and pimping at dog shows.

A brief history lesson: Dogs shows began in England in the nineteenth century as agriculture shows at which hunting dogs were judged to determine which dog was the best. In time, the "ladies' dogs" were exhibited, and dog shows were headed on the road to Oz. Straight men resented that the women had dogs at all. "Miniature spaniels? Toy terriers? Useless lap dogs!" cried the he-man upland game hunter. Soon the queers would steal his duck-toting Poodle from beneath his very boots.

Gay men transformed the dog show in America from an informal ladies' sport to a more intense, higher level competition. The American way of showing dogs today is highly charged by gay energy—think beauty pageant with four-legged contestants and no hooters. The handlers dress smartly and professionally, although we're not taking credit for any of the women's shoes. The dogs are conditioned, trained, and groomed to the nines. A dog show is no longer a sideshow at the county fair: it is a show with the production values of a Broadway musical.

Think of the grandeur and spectacle that is the Westminster Kennel Club Dog Show in New York City. No matter what the "in-crowd" says about the show, it's a black-tie affair. It's professional and it's an event. The level of the handlers'

What's So Gay About a Dog Show?

The author interviewed a top-winning Non-Sporting dog for the following passage. This particular dog, a proud member of the Bichon Frisé breed, did not *whisper* any of this to me: he fairly bellowed it in my ear.

Bitches, it's show time! Get the girls and the boys dolled up. Shampoo, rinse, repeat. Fluff those coats, comb out those topknots. Blow dryer blowing fuses.

Enter the big ring. All eyes on me as I sashay the first time around. Find a place to pose. Freeze-frame: he's watching me. Attitude, attitude. Daddy, give me that bait. Pose, cock the head, look alert but not too interested. He knows I want it bad. Pouf me up: stroke, stroke.

One more time around the room, sashay, sashay. Glance at the gallery. They love me. They want me. He's watching me walk.

Stand very still. He's touching my teeth (that's odd), and now he's fondling my privates. He's all mine. At dog shows, the prettiest boys (and girls) win.

Another lucky night, and I got the ribbon and a photo with the guy to prove it.

Best in Show

professionalism at American shows such as Westminster and the Beverly Hills Kennel Club is lavender with a twist. The flair is unmistakable; sometimes it's bejeweled and brocaded (like a certain fabulous sequin-jacketed professional who stole the Hound Group in the mid-1990s). Year after year, gay men circle the Best in Show ring, usually taking home the ribbons and silver cups.

There's a certain queerness involved in showmanship of this caliber. It's a craft, a talent, a calling. How many straight boys are dancing on Broadway or at the American Ballet Theatre? Gay men fuel Broadway's creativity, and this same energy is evident in the dog-show world.

Attend any major all-breed dog show, and observe the lineup in the group ring. Of course there are more gays in the Toy and Non-Sporting Groups, which *not coincidentally* are the two most competitive groups. Likely, the most magnificent dogs with hair down to the floor have been dolled up by gay men, who are proudly presenting them with professional panache. A good many of them have bred the dogs as well.

The author is not suggesting that gay men transformed the glamour breeds *single-handedly*; no, in fact, they used both hands. One such ambidextrous dog man, David Murray, is a talented groomer, breeder, handler, and Hollywood hairstylist, and he testifies to his attraction to the "glamorous life" of show dogs.

> I always loved the look and glamour of breeds like the Lhasa or Maltese. . . . In 1988 I went to a show and saw my first Tibetan Terrier and was instantly attracted. This wasn't a particularly glamorous dog, just a cute, fuzzy, medium-sized "Benji"-type dog. I quickly went from just wanting this type of dog as a pet to realizing that, if I put some effort behind this, I could make one of these into a successful show dog. With my experience as a hairstylist, and a good working knowledge of the sport in general from when I was a kid, I set out with the lofty goal of making a Tibetan Terrier a top winner. To me, my greatest satisfaction comes from taking a young hopeful puppy and seeing it through maturity, both mentally and physically, to the beautiful end result of a top show Tibetan Terrier.

David Murray has become one of the top breeders and handlers in the dog sport and holds the record for most Best in Show wins for a Tibetan Terrier.

The question lingers, what does a man's sexual preference have to do with his ability to groom an Afghan Hound? Perhaps there are "gay genes" that trigger these creative powers, powers that inspire and bring about the "creation of beauty." Many gay men have a natural sense of beauty. Writing music, poetry, drama; directing musicals and operas; arranging flowers; creating hairstyles;

From Beehives and Bouffants to Best in Show

Ken Sinclair of the world-renowned Araki Tibetan Terriers tells us the story of how it all happened:

> I have always loved dogs, especially Afghan Hounds as they are so unique and flashy; you often saw them in the papers and glossy magazines dotted around the models of the day. As a young lad I was a hippie, part of the Flower Power generation. I had long hair then with my Afghan coat and moon boots, and I was certainly noticed walking my two Afghan Hounds whilst trolling along the seafront. I trained as a hairdresser because all my friends were doing the same, and I managed to get the odd day off to get away to show my dogs. It wasn't too long, however, before I upgraded to dog beautician, a move from one sort of bitch to another, so to speak! I was never a good hairdresser anyway, fabulous at back-combing as in those days everyone wanted a beehive whether they were ten or ninety years of age. Coloring I never could get right, although some of the colors I ended up with were *spectacular,* to say the least, just not what the client had asked for! My perming was disastrous as again they always looked like Standard Poodles. So on my first hairdressing job they paid me six months' leave on the understanding I would *not* come into the salon again.
>
> So I moved on and went to work full time in a kennel, and I took my three Afghans with me. The kennel owner owned Afghans but also had Tibetan Terriers, and I found my true talent in preparing these dogs for shows. I soon made this my full-time profession and am proud to say I have been successful in both breeds, although now I am noted for my Tibetan Terriers. I have also become a successful English and international champion show judge. I have made many friends in the dog world, some closer than others (especially in my younger, more hedonistic days), but I now attend the shows with my partner, Neil Smith, who has a more steadying influence on my fiery Scottish temper.

designing dresses; grooming Afghans; breeding Maltese, Poodles, and Whippets . . . these all evoke the creation of beauty, and they are among the powers of gay men. Or, perhaps, it's all coincidental.

Visit a dog show and experience the spectacle yourself. At outdoor shows, you are able to enter the show grounds with a dog who's not entered in the show. This will be an eye-opening experience. You may even meet a few cute handlers. If you want to strike up a conversation, ask them about "ringside pickups." If you want to enter your dog in a show, it's simple enough to do. Your dog has to be registered with the kennel club (e.g., AKC, CKC) sponsoring the show, and the dog has to be unaltered. You can go online and enter the show through the American Kennel Club or the hosting show-giving organization.

Dog showing can be entertaining and enjoyable for novices, especially well-dressed young guys with well-trained dogs. Wear fitted slacks and a solid-colored sports coat; do not wear jeans or sneakers, even to an outdoor show. You want to make a favorable impression on the judge.

If you're lucky enough to get a gay male judge in your ring, you may make the first cut (as the judge will probably want to watch you sashay around his ring again and this time pay attention to the puppy's gait instead of yours). It is perfectly acceptable to smile at the judge and show interest in everything he's saying and doing (even if it's a female judge). You're well advised not to pass your telephone number to the judge until *after* the judge has pointed his finger and made his placements. Whatever you do, don't let the ring steward see you passing the note (he could be the judge's lover or, worse, an AKC delegate from a red state!).

A LITTLE BRAINS, A LITTLE TALENT

Beyond dog shows, there are many activities that owners and dogs can pursue, although some of these could result in a bruised ego and a broken nail (yours, not the dog's). All of these competitions require that Lola the Wonder Toy be trained to the nines, not just dressed that way. Although you may be able to charm your way to an Award of Merit at a dog show, your graces and good looks won't propel your Beagle over the high jump. Here's a rundown of what's available in the dog-world circuit and some advice about each.

Obedience Trials

Have you actually taught that dog to sit yet? If so, you may want to kick it up a notch, and try your hand at competitive obedience, which is based on achieving high scores in exercises that demonstrate the dog's knowledge of basic and advanced training. You will be able to get your Papillon through the Companion Dog level with relative ease, but you'll really have to buckle down to get through the Utility class. If you have a stubborn breed, or one that's too smart for training, obedience will probably not be much fun.

Agility Trials

These trials are like obstacle courses for really smart, fast dogs. They're a lot more interesting to watch than obedience trials. Who wants to watch ten dogs staring into space for three minutes? Agility trials are as entertaining as Olympic luge or curling events, although not as silly. Agility trials are dominated by Border Collies and other push-button canines. Don't torture your Frenchie or Maltese by trying to get him to climb an A-frame or run through a plastic tunnel. Poodles, not surprisingly, do very well . . . bitches! They have brains *and* beauty.

Tracking Tests

It's handy to train your dog to follow his nose, formally known as tracking. He'll be able to find the glove you lost at the ball or the troll who swiped your *Vanity Fair* at the beach. Tracking dogs can even catch escaped convicts, criminals, runaway daddies, and other tough bad boys—we should really start looking into renting Bloodhounds for the weekend.

Earthdog Trials

Terriers and Dachshunds tunnel into holes to locate trapped vermin. Despite what you're thinking, lesbians aren't the only ones at these trials, but most of the gay men are discreet and dress up in drab coats and baseball caps to blend in with the ladies.

Flyball

Team relays over hurdles—fast, furious, and fun. Basically as much fun as can possibly be had with eight dogs and two tennis balls!

Rally-O

This is a cross between obedience and agility that is ideal for newcomers to the dog sport. A course is set up, using between ten and twenty exercises. Signs are set up around the course, each of which tells you what to do with the dog. None of the signs says "Vogue" or "Just stare at me," so this is obviously more fun for the dog than the handler.

Herding Trials

Cattle and chickens and ducks, oh my! You name it, a herding dog can make it retreat into a pen. If you like chasing chickens, this is the sport for you and your Aussie. However, if you have an inexplicable fear of goats and other woolly livestock, stay on the other side of the gate.

Lure Coursing

For the sighthound set, these trials attract owners of Italian Greyhounds and retired Greyhounds and everyone in between. It doesn't sound that interesting to watch a Whippet chase down a plastic bag across a field in the rain, but the dogs twitter like it's college night at the Crowbar.

Weight Pulls

A sport for Bears and the Pump Boys, this is a muscle-dog event in which the dogs pull heavy loads over a specified distance. Huskies do well in this, too, but they'd rather be pulling sleds in Aspen. For the rest of us, weight pulling is a little more exciting than darts at a redneck gin mill.

Field Trials and Coonhound Events

Ladies, puuuhlease! These trials are work, not fun. Rigorous training in all kinds of weather, a truly dismal wardrobe, and dead animals galore. Sure, the retrievers love it, but they also love rolling in cat puke in the backyard. And, if you think a night hunt in Atlanta sounds scintillating, you are barking up the wrong tree.

Dancing with Dogs

Somewhere out there is a gay contingent for this quasi-sport, looking to mold "doggy freestyle" from a troupe of housewives flouncing around to "Flashdance" to the Fabulous Fosse Frenchies high stepping to "Steam Heat" or the Balanchine Boxers in the "Slaughter on Tenth Avenue" ballet. Of course, for a doggy two-step or line dance, you can count on an irrepressible crew of Cowgirls and retro 'mos in the wings ready to kick it to "Achy Breaky Heart." Check out the World Canine Freestyle Organization on the Web.

STONEWOOF

Not only do homosexuals have more rights and liberties in European countries such as Sweden and Finland, but so do the dogs! Indeed the Maple Leaf Fags and their dogs in Canada have it better than gays and their dogs in the United States. A question arises: did the Puritans fear dogs the way they feared queers? Why then are dogs so downtrodden in the United States? In Europe, a well-behaved dog can travel anywhere, eat in restaurants, and run on the beaches; he is genuinely regarded as a member of the family. American dogs are banned from most public places and are treated like third-class citizens or noncitizens. In some places, you can be fined if your dog barks!

It's time to set the stage for Stonewoof! Let's raise our voices and lift our legs all over Sheridan Square one more time! Instead of passing laws to ban "dangerous dogs" in our communities, let's pass laws to ban stupid dog owners or make some strides at educating or deporting them. We can start by becoming model dog owners: keeping our dogs on leashes when in public, cleaning up after them, and training them to behave properly. Consider working toward a Canine Good Citizen certificate, an AKC program that promotes responsible ownership.

It seems that most local politicians were terrorized by nasty Cocker Spaniels when they were children, hence all of the "no-dogs" legislation. How sad is it that you can't take a retriever to most beaches in the country? Who enjoys the surf more than a Golden Retriever chasing a stick? Even a Cali Boy tires after a few throws. In some communities, off-leash dog parks are prohibited due to strictly enforced leash laws. Off-leash advocates have become very vocal recently and have organized in cities across the continent. (Visit www.thebark.com to hear the cries of some of them.) Organized efforts for political action have yielded leash-free parks in Berkeley, Brooklyn, Manhattan, Portland, San Diego, San Francisco, and Seattle. SFDOG in San Francisco, COLA in Seattle, Dog PAC in Santa Barbara, and NYCDOG in New York City are some of the groups leading the way. If you (and your dog) are sick of being tied up or down, get involved with a political-action group and let loose.

It's equally devastating to accept that psychotic individuals have ruined the bulldog from *Our Gang*. Did Spanky and Alfalfa ever have a problem with Petey? American Pit Bull Terriers, called bulldogs by the old-timers, are as American as apple pie, musical comedy, and gay Cowboys. Breed-specific legislation aimed at "pit-bulls and similar breeds" will never solve the problem of irresponsible owners neglecting their dogs until they become dangerous, unpredictable, or vicious. The number of measures proposed nationwide is on the rise, so dog owners should be more vigilant about what's happening in their own communities. The AKC stands up against these measures and thus far has a good track record of dissuading the courts from passing breed-specific laws. Everyone knows that Cockers and Chihuahuas bite more people annually than Pit Bulls. Once the precedent is set, the breed bans will go from Pit Bulls to Bull Terriers to Boston Terriers, then trickle down to Cockers, Yorkies, and on and on. Be responsible, train your dog, and let your representatives know that you love your Bully pal and that you vote.

Although we're not setting out to author the doggy Bill of Rights, there are so many wrongs in our country done to our "best friends" that it's time we speak up for the voiceless. On the eve of Stonewoof, we'll be able to take our Poodles to dinner, play with them on the beach, and maybe even take them to the Monster for happy hour.

CHARITY WORK

You don't have to be Mrs. Astor or Mrs. Rockefeller Dodge to raise your goblet at a charity ball. Since the onset of AIDS, gay men's social calendars have been beveled with charity events. If we're not attending a preview of the newest Bill Finn musical for GMHC, we're writing checks at local charity galas, silent auctions, and champagne brunches. Dog owners may also find themselves hobnobbing with other Ladies of Leisure at an SPCA, Delta Society, or PAWS program. Contributing time and effort to bettering the communities in which we live improves our lives and the lives of everyone around us, including our dogs.

Some charity events are ideal for dogs; in fact, you would think a few dogs were on the committee that invented the walk-a-thon. AIDS walks continue to raise millions annually in cities large and small, and our four-legged pals are right by our sides.

If you're looking to share your dog with those less fortunate, you can become a therapy team that visits nursing homes, children's hospitals, and other facilities. Therapy dogs need nothing more than basic obedience, a smiling temperament, a waggy tail, and an owner whose Fossil keeps good time. Therapy dogs can also visit special-education classes and kids with other handicaps. Autistic children and children who have been traumatized physically or emotionally can benefit exponentially from the soft muzzle and friendly paw of a therapy dog.

To volunteer as a therapy team, you can approach facilities on your own or pursue the more formal route of getting your dog certified as an official Therapy Dog. The Pet Partners Program of the Delta Society aims to ensure that both dog and handler are properly prepared to participate in animal-assisted therapy. They require volunteer training and screening of dog-handler teams. Nearly 1 million people benefit from the PPP volunteers in all fifty states and Canada.

You can also volunteer to work with one of the community service groups that assist pet owners living with AIDS. Among the services offered by these groups are dog walking, pet transportation, grooming, litter box changing, and foster care. In some cases, the groups help to rehome the pets if it becomes necessary. POWARS in New York City was one of the first of these groups. Some of the best known groups today are PAWS in San Francisco, PALS in Atlanta, PETS-DC in Washington, D.C., the Delta Society in Renton, Washington, and Action AIDS in Philadelphia.

Of course, volunteering for a local animal shelter as a dog walker or kennel assistant is rewarding for many dog owners and other dog-loving people. Others get more involved and become foster homes for abandoned dogs, while rescue groups help find permanent homes. In New York City, a wonderful fund-raising event called Broadway Barks was started by Broadway dog trainer Bill Berloni. With the assistance of two of the great ladies of the stage and major gay icons, Bernadette Peters and Mary Tyler Moore, as well as most of the casts on Broadway, the event raises thousands of dollars each year and finds homes for hundreds of dogs in an afternoon.

Now that dogs have gone from gutter to glamour, the well-dressed canine is on the runway of fashion shows on both coasts. The worlds of high fashion and queer dogs collide on the catwalk at doggy fashion shows being

Take the Lead

Dog handlers, judges, and breeders responded to the devastating toll that the AIDS crisis was having on the dog fancy by establishing Take the Lead in 1993. Many top dog men were afflicted, and the challenge of their care and well-being was met by the caring individuals that established this nonprofit organization. Since its inception, Take the Lead has expanded its scope from people living with HIV/AIDS to victims of other ruthless diseases, including cancer. Fund-raisers and the support of the AKC, its member clubs, and kennel clubs have made it possible for the organization to assist afflicted individuals in the dog fancy and beyond. Take the Lead well deserves the support of everyone in the dog fancy, as the organization continues to provide direct services, support, and care for the dog lovers who make up the sport of purebred dogs.

held in the major cities on both coasts. *Animal Fair Magazine* presents its annual "Paws for Style" in Manhattan and Hollywood for the elite of café society and the canine chic. These slick events attract celebrities, high-fashion models (bi- and quadruped), hounds and media hounds, and lots of homos and their best girlfriends. New York's Pet Fashion Week climaxes in a doggy fashion show of inspiring heights, a black-tie event accompanied by an art exhibition and a silent auction, all raising funds for some dog-eared charity. Unless you know the doorman or make the A list, you probably won't be able to sneak your pup into one of these events. But at least once you get home, sloppy, plastered, and a bit poorer, you can say you did it for the dogs.

VACATIONS

After working fifty weeks a year, you deserve a real vacation to escape the responsibilities of the real world. Your trusty Lukas or little Brad hangs around day after day, waiting for you to get a day off to spend some quality time with him, and what do you do? You board him at a kennel or send him to Camp Bow Wow so you can frolic *au naturel* at a nudist camp in Palm Springs. Even though doggy day care for a week can be a health spa for a dog—and Camp Bow Wow has video monitors!—Lukas would rather be with you, showing off *his* shapely buttocks and well-tucked abdomen in Southern California or Key West (or wherever!). A not-so-innocent guilt-free week away with your dog is the perfect gin and tonic for the world-weary queer traveler.

Gay Resorts and Bed & Breakfasts

Touring around North America with your four-legged pal can be as easy as clicking your heels three times. It will require more planning to go to Europe or Oz (Australia, not Munchkinland). Before booking a week at the hottest gay B&B on the coast, find out if the guesthouse accepts dogs. You would be surprised to find out how many gay-owned and -operated resorts and B&Bs accept dogs. From Fort La-dee-dah to Toront-homo, gay men and their dogs have an array of swank lodging options. Should you be looking for sun and fun or ice and dice, you can find it in Puerta Vallarta and Atlanta or Anchorage and Las Vegas. There are some great gay travel guides available online and in print. The *Spartacus International Gay Guide,* updated annually, continues to be gay men's most reliable travel "dicktionary"—always worth cruising and perusing. The *Damron Men's Travel Guide* will also give you good up-to-date information on gay travel. Neither guide offers any information on pet-friendly accommodations, so pick up the phone and give your intended hotel a call. Some guesthouses and hotels will accept dogs, and you might even be able to find a tea dance or beach party that's open to pets. Most dogs don't care for club music or saunas anyway, so yours won't mind staying at the hotel while you check out the bar, bath, and behinds.

Visit Pet Friendly Vacation Rentals at www.petvr.com to find current listings of houses, cabins, villas, and chateaus available for rent, all of which are dog friendly. Pick the queerest village or swankiest gay city on the map (North America, Europe, and beyond), and you and your four-legged partner will be booked in fine accommodations. Whether your sights are set on Provincetown, Key West, Laguna Beach, or Blowing Rock, North Carolina (it exists, I swear), you will find it here. So if those little black books of gay travel don't give you the dog info you require, go online and book your vacation with your pooch.

Road Trips and Pet Fests

Here's a real "Q" American notion: pack up the Yorkie, stack up the Streisand and dance tunes, and rack up the miles on your Hummer. It's a gay road trip, boys! This is the kind of tour that would make Jack Kerouac puke, although the brass at Exxon/Mobil think it's swell. "See America First" and then do them. Life's highway is a one-way street and, as Jean-Paul Sartre wrote, "No exit. No shoulder."

When I first heard about Hawaii Fi-Do, a doggy festival, even my tail was wagging! Visions of riding mai tais and sipping surfers swelled in my head. Bring an ice pack for Martha the Yorkie, and she'll cope fine with a tropical heat wave. Then the wave crashed! Hawaii Fi-Do is in Madison, Wisconsin. That's not the sunny South Pacific, that's Lake Superior. No one writes musicals about Wisconsin. Why would my Yorkie want to go there?

Martha voted yes, and 2,000 miles later the Hummer was eating my AmEx card alive. Madison in June was paradise, and we felt the warmth of the Midwest. The Hawaii/Wisconsin one featured wacky pet contests, musical chairs, doggy survivor (don't ask), training demos (the Yorkie abstained), a pet parade, flyball, a microchip clinic, and much more. (We passed out after the injection.) You don't have to drive across the country to attend a dog festival, however; they're being staged and sponsored all over the continent.

For dog lovers who've always dreamed of going over the falls, how about the Niagara DogFest in August of each year? You and your buddy can participate in all kinds of four-legged fun, including training and new product demonstrations, contests, a nail-cutting clinic, groomers' forums, and lots of shopping with vendors from near and far selling far-out fancy pooch amenities. Oh, yeah, and there's always Steamworks in Toronto to show off your new tan lines.

You can plan your vacation schedule around the pet festivals—think "Snowbird" and take little Annie-M to Florida for the holiday parties. There are many one-day events catering to canines, offering doggy goody bags, games, and contests. Plus, while you're in the Swamp State, you can take in the sights. Nothing can evoke the mood of the holiday better than watching the palm trees sway . . . on a cabana boy's bikini! For a real Americana road trip, how about tea dance in Boston, the site of the original tea party? The city on the harbor has much to offer gay owners and their pups. How about treating yourself and Barry the hound dog to a weekend in New England? Although Mrs. Astor's staff won't allow Barry into Beechwood, there are plenty of outdoor sights to enjoy.

If you want to leave the Hummer home, then don't overlook Dog Island, Florida, as a possible getaway. South of Carrabelle on the Panhandle, it's an actual island, small, remote, and dog-friendly, as the name denotes. You and Ginger will arrive by boat, plane, or ferry. Dogs are welcome on the beach (provided they're leashed). While the nightlife isn't going to rival Duval Street, this is a peaceful resort possibility, with no chance of Ginger being spotted by the paparazzi, although you may meet a shipwrecked mariner hard on his luck.

And if you're looking for real "family" entertainment, don't forget gay Disney in Orlando and Anaheim. Three cheers for Minnie and the Mousekequeers! A true gay-friendly corporation.

Low Camp: Into the Woods

Camping with dogs can be gayer than you think. Gay campsites, where the boys erect their own tents and much more, have been popular weekend escapes around the country. Bringing your dog to a campsite can be a terrific weekend bonding with your dog and other new friends. As Dorothy found out, the forest presents many dangers to little dogs, including ticks and other itchy parasites, water pollutants, and wild animals. In the summer months, heat stroke kills many dogs. Be sure your dog has access to clean water all of the time. A canteen is a neat accessory to attach to your belt or fanny pack. Don't let your dog drink water from the stream or river. Keep a close eye on your dog the whole time you're in the woods. Your dog's safety has to remain your main focus, no matter how alluring the Colt model in the next tent.

Campsites have many challenging activities for dogs and the owners. Fetching in a stream, fishing, and canoeing are just the beginning. If your dog's not a seasoned swimmer, invest in a life vest for him. If you have a real Sporting breed, and a straight friend or family member who's not afraid of flying monkeys, you can consider hunting with little Toto. Retrievers, pointers, setters, spaniels, and scenthounds love to get their noses full of wildlife and follow their noses. Hunting is a passion for all of these dogs and manly men who pursue this sort of thing. It's not on the top of most gay men's lists of fabulous things to do on weekends, but for many dogs it's natural and exhilarating.

If taking to the woods with your dog seems beyond your gay scope, consider a dog camp. Sort of like summer camp without bratty children, a dog camp is an organized week- or weekend-long event. Dogs and their owners can try their paws at crafts, sports, and games. Different camps offer different activities, but the possibilities are endless, including flyball, agility, racing, and swimming. Every dog is welcome to try every event, so if you've always thought your Pekingese would enjoy a terrier race, this is your chance to bet the Peke stakes. Canine camps are available in every region of the country and have Web sites with scheduling and other information. Not every dog enjoys the dog-on-dog experience that these camps offer, but some dogs are naturally competitive and love the challenge. For other dogs and their dads, time spent at picnic tables with lunch pails, Miller Lite, and macramé might be the perfect doggy getaway.

The Slippery Slopes

If you have a Nordic breed such as a Siberian Husky or an Alaskan Malamute, you certainly should consider winter sports with your dog. Any athletic double-coated dog would be willing to comply. Although catching snowballs is entertaining, there's a whole white world out there for skiers and skijorers. Taking your dog along to Aspen, Stowe, or even Zurich would be a real vacation. The ski resort in Vancouver (called Whistler) has a gay week every February. To skijor with the dog, you need a harness, a special belt, and a pair of skis (for you). You can begin the dog's training at home with roller skates, a small cart, or a bike. Once your Husky gets on snow, he'll amaze you with his natural talent and love of the sport. Few things are as uplifting as the mountains, the driven snow, and a wet-nosed chalet chum.

Water Sports

After you've overcome those embarrassing marking incidents, your dog may be ready for some real water sports. California jills know the joy of Jeeping to the shore with their Golden Retrievers in tow and having a barking audience on the beach as they're riding the swell. If surfing for you is only a grand spectator sport, how about swimming, canoeing, or sailing? Even a retriever or a water dog such as the Irish Water Spaniel needs to be introduced to water, so be sure that he's comfortable with getting his paws wet before expecting him to join in the water. Don't forget to vest up the dog, too. Doggy life vests are essential when taking your dog on the water. For beachcombers who aren't so adventuresome, take your dog for a shell-collecting tour on the beach. In your itsy-bitsy Armani thong, you may pick up more than a conch. According to www.americasbestonline.net, these are America's top ten pet-friendly beaches in order:

St. George Island, Florida: Across the bay from historic Apalachicola, this twenty-nine-mile island has fabulous vacation homes, great seafood eats, and lenient leash laws.

Dog Beach, California: Located near San Diego, Ocean Beach's Dog Beach is for dog owners and their dogs.

Cape San Blas, Florida: East of Panama City on the Gulf Coast, this twenty-mile beach is dog friendly and private in the off-season.

Carmel City Beach, California: One of three pet-friendly beaches near Carmel, it is worth a gander for a gay goose and his sporty dog. The other two are Carmel River State Beach and Garrapata State Park. Dogs who listen can be unleashed.

Dog Island, Florida: Located on the well-named Dog Island, south of Carrabelle and fifty miles east of Panama City, Dog Park Beach is sunny, sandy, and friendly.

Hunting Island, South Carolina: Rent a cabin for you, your Southern Belle, and your hound on Hunting Island and enjoy four miles of lovely dog-friendly beach in this park.

Jekyll Island, Georgia: On Jekyll Island, you find trails and beaches where dogs are welcome. If you're headed into the woods in the warm months, bring bug spray and don't wear your Guccis on the dirt trails.

Grayton Beach State Recreation Area, Florida: Dogs are welcome in some areas of this oceanfront park.

Pistol River State Scenic Viewpoint, Oregon: Check out the dogs and their windsurfing daddies south of Gold Beach. You'll find great views all around this park.

Fort Fisher State Recreation Area, North Carolina: Head for the southern tip of Pleasure Island (!!). Dogs aren't allowed on the beaches with lifeguards, so you'll swim and sunbathe at your own risk (and keep your eyes peeled for an off-duty hottie).

PARTY HOUNDS AND CIRCUIT PUPS

A White Party is no place for a furry creature on all fours! It's quite uncommon to see any dog on the circuit—bunnies, bears, and chickens for certain, but no dogs allowed. The weekend party crowd leaves the dogs at home or in a dog-friendly hotel in the city. Most dogs would be distressed by the flashing lights, the loud music, and the sight of their owners in collars.

An indulgent resort in Palm Springs or a weekend in Cherry Grove on Fire Island might be as close as your pooch wants to get to the boy party that's calling your name. Keep him out of the dunes, as he's bound to pick up some itchy critter that's hard to get rid of—and likely so are you.

If you've got your heart set on New Orleans's ever-gay Mardi *Grrrr* in February, Palm Springs's White Party in April, Provincetown's Carnival Week in August, or Fort Lauderdale's White Party in November, you can book a pet-friendly guesthouse in any of those towns by visiting www.petvr.com.

After a hot summer and endless beach parties, the autumn is always welcome. Fags love the fall, and October is the gayest month. Deciding where to go in this great month is a real queer quandary. Packing up your cha-cha heels for the Black and Blue Festival in Montreal promises bruises to last a lifetime, while Key West's fagtastic Fantasy Fest turns the island lavender for days. Of course, the Halloween parades in the Village or the Castro are dog-friendly holidays for the whole family, although only adult dogs should attend. A young, impressionable puppy could be scarred for life by a nine-foot Drag Queen parading as Kelly Clarkson.

GROOMING SHOWS

The early 1970s were marked by big hair on both ends of the leash. A beehive or a bushy moustache and a Poodle combed out to the Lord. Many gays found religion standing behind a salon chair or grooming table: the higher the hair, the closer to Jesus. Grooming shows may be even more gay than dog shows, as these events oxidize all "G" elements into one astonishing spectacle. One of the first and surely longest running grooming shows takes place in Illinois, the All American Grooming Show, shepherded by groomer turned actor turned dog breeder/exhibitor turned showman Jerry Schinberg. These industry-focused exhibitions give dog groomers a place to "strut their stuff" so that other groomers can learn from the top dog beauticians and find out about innovative products. The creative styling of dogs exhibited at these shows involves not only unconventional trims, such as the Cowboy and the Carousel Horse, but also colors. Bless those Poodles who withstand the heights and depths of the queer imagination. Some groomers get so carried away that they involve costumes, sets, and soundtracks. Lots of Rodgers and Hammerstein wafting from the Poodle exhibits. To be fair, lots of helpful education goes on at these shows, too, and these events have become indispensable forums for groomers to learn the intricacies of the various coated breeds.

Other grooming shows around the country include Intergroom on the East Coast, which features guest speakers, educational seminars, best-in-show contests, a trade show, and, recently, an "extreme makeover" for a dog. In the Southeast, there's the Atlanta Pet Fair, a pet-stylist extravaganza, trade show, and competition. Visit www.petgroomer.com for a complete listing of grooming shows in the United States.

JUNE IS BUSTING OUT

Gay parades and pridefests spangle the North American map during the summer months. You and your rainbow pup could jet, Amtrak, or motor from every corner each weekend and be soaking in the gay sun week after week. Think of all of the towns that you can paint pink. From New York to

Montreal to Boston to Miami to Atlanta to Seattle to San Francisco to Austin to Toronto—and that's just June—you'd be one tired-out puppy with holes in your hot pants. Because parades and pride-fests are outdoor events, dogs are most often welcome spectators and even participants. A few years ago in Hotlanta, a gander of gay boys dyed their Standard Poodles into a rainbow of canine pride. For those unconvinced that Poodles were the gayest breed, this display of warped homo pride closed the case. Some of the Poodles even had hair higher than RuPaul's!

Dress your pup in a rainbow bandana or a lavender (or mauve) bow tie, something to complement your tasteful slinkiness. Prowling with your gay little dog, meeting new faces, and inadvertently brushing up against thousands of sweaty male bods sums up the meaning of community pride.

Whenever your dog is out in public, be sure to have his leash attached and all of his identification information securely fastened to his collar. The festivities can sometimes be overwhelming for man and dog alike, so keep your pal's safety in mind.

Once you've found the perfect canine companion, the whole gay world is your oyster. Sunning at the shore, sipping at the rim of an overpriced cocktail, and watching the surfers come in, you and your partner can woof all day at the indescribable joys of low tide. Here's hoping every day is a beach day! Cheers!